동지중해의
결혼 문화와 전통

Eastern Mediterranean Marriage Culture and Traditions

동지중해의
결혼 문화와 전통

지중해지역원 지음

이 저서는 2018년 대한민국 교육부와 한국연구재단의 지원을 받아 수행된 연구임
(NRF-2018S1A6A3A02022221)

프롤로그

동지중해의 결혼 문화와 전통
(Eastern Mediterranean Marriage Culture and Traditions)

윤용수

인간은 출생한 시점부터 사망에 이르기까지 인생의 항해를 하면서 많은 과정과 단계를 거치기 마련이다. 독일 출신의 민족학자인 아놀드 반 게넵(A. Van Gennep, 1873~1957)은 인생의 행로 중 모든 인간에게 예외없이 적용되는 단계를 '출생-성장-결혼-사망'으로 구분하고 이를 '인생의 통과의례(通過儀禮, rite of passage)'란 용어로 표현했다.

위의 4가지 통과의례 중 출생, 성장과 사망은 인간의 의지가 아닌 자연 또는 신의 영역이기 때문에 비선택적·불가항력적 항목이라면 결혼은 인간 자신의 의지로 결정할 수 있는 유일한 선택적 항목이라 하겠다.

이러한 결혼의 특성과 중요성 때문에 인간의 올바른 삶과 방향 제시를 주요 기능으로 하는 인류의 주요 보편 종교에서도 결혼의 중요성과 당위성에 대해 공통적으로 강조하고 있다. 성서의 창세기에서는 아담의 탄생에 이어 이브의 탄생을 언급하고 있고, 두 사람의 결혼을 하나님이 주신 선물로 묘사하고 있다. 이슬람교의 경전인 꾸란에서도 여러 곳에 걸쳐 올바른 결혼과 남편과 아내의 역할을 언급하고 있고, 사도 무함마드의 언행록인 하디스(Hadith)에서는 결혼을 '종교의 절반'으로 묘사하며 결혼을 무슬림의 종교적 의무로 규정하고 있다.

이처럼 동지중해 지역의 대표 종교인 기독교와 이슬람교에서는 결혼을 하나님의 축복이며 사랑과 신뢰에 기초한 아름다운 결합으로 묘사하고 있지만, 현실 사회에서 결혼은 기본적으로 정치적 · 사회적 · 경제적 요인들이 주요 변수로 작용한 인간 사회의 제도이자 관습이며, 그 속성상 결혼은 집단 간 계약의 성격이 강하다.

결혼은 인류의 역사와 그 궤적을 같이 해 오면서 시대, 자연환경, 사회적 조건, 남녀 성비 등의 변수에 따라 시대별, 지역별로 다양하게 발전해 왔다. 결혼은 남녀 당사자의 성적(性的), 심리적, 경제적인 결합인 동시에 사회의 기초 단위인 가정을 구성할 뿐만 아니라, 종족 보전을 위한 둥지를 제공하기도 한다. 아울러 결혼을 통해서 정치, 경제, 외교적 협력과 제휴를 하기도 하는 등 결혼은 남녀의 만남 이상의 주요한 사회적 기능을 수행해 왔기 때문에, 모든 인간 공동체는 어떤 형태로든 결혼에 대한 다양한 제도와 방식 및 규제를 마련해 왔다.

인류 역사에서 결혼은 집단혼(group marriage)으로 시작되었고, 한 혈족의 형제 자매와 다른 혈족의 형제 자매가 교차하여서 짝을 짓는 결혼 방식인 대우혼(對偶婚)을 거쳐 일부일처제가 보편적인 결혼 방식으로 정착되었다.

배우자의 범위는 원시 사회에서는 형제-자매간의 결혼이 일반적이었으나, 점차 배우자의 선택 범위는 친척→씨족→부족 등으로 확대되어 갔다. 하지만 원시 형태의 국가가 만들어지고 권력 구조가 생성된 이후에 사회 상층부를 구성하는 권력 계층은 그들의 권력과 부의 누수를 방지하기 위해 친족간의 족내혼을 우선하기도 했다.

성서에 등장하는 아브라함의 아내 사라는 아브라함의 이복동생이고 이집트 신화에 등장하는 오시리스(Osiris)의 아내 이시스(Isis) 역시 오시리스의 이복 동생이다. 이슬람에서는 지금도 사촌간의 결혼을 허용하고 있다. 이처럼 원시 사회에서는 근친 결혼이 불가피했던 측면이 있지만, 결혼을 권력과 부의 유지 및 확장의 수단으로 사용한 측면도 있다.

인류의 역사 발전 과정은 결혼의 형태에도 영향을 미쳤다. 인류 공동체가 수렵 채집 사회에 머물러 있던 신석기 시대는 모계 중심사회였고 일처다부제가 일반적이었다. 수렵은 주로 남자들의 몫이었고 채집은 여성들의 몫이었다. 수렵은 불안정했지만 채집은 안정적으로 유지될 수 있었기 때문에 여성들의 영향력이 컸고 자연스럽게 모계 중심의 일처다부제가 만들어 졌다.

21세기에 감소하는 추세지만 히말라야 지역의 부탄왕국이나 티베트, 중국 서부와 인도의 일부 지역에서는 여전히 일처다부제가 유지되고 있다. 이는 토지와 재산의 유출을 막고 효과적인 가족 집단 운영을 위해서 남자 형제들이 한 명의 여자와 결혼하는 풍습이 유지되고 있는 것이다. 일처다부제 가정에서 아내는 잠자리를 할 남편을 선택할 수 있었고, 부부사이에서 태어난 자식의 아버지를 공개하지 않음으로써 공동체의 안정과 평화를 유지하고 있다. 일처다부제 사회에서 가정의 권한은 당연히 여성에게 주어진 것이다.

인류 사회가 수렵 채집 사회에서 농경 사회로 발전하면서 가계 경제에서 남자의 노동력이 보다 중요해졌다. 농경 정착 사회에서는 노동력이 중시된다. 남자는 여자에 비해 노동력이 우월함에 따라 가족 내에서 남성을 중시하게 되어 남성의 영향력은 자연스럽게 커졌다. 이는 모계 사회를 부계 중심 사회로 변화시키는 주요 원인이 되었다.

가족내에서 남녀의 역할과 주도권 향방에 따라 가족의 체계와 힘의 구조도 함께 변화한 것이다. 이에 따라 결혼제도도 일처다부제에서 일부다처제로 변화했다. 이 변화는 부계 상속제의 정착으로 이어지면서 남성 중심의 부계 중심 사회가 시작된 것이다.

부계 상속제 사회에서는 아버지와 남자 자식의 혈통이 중요했기 때문에 남편은 아내에게 본인 이외의 남자와의 성관계를 금지시키며 여성의 정절을 요구하는 문화가 만들어졌다. 아내는 정절의 의무를 지키는 대가로 정처(正妻)로서의 지위와 자신이 낳은 아들에게 재산 상속을 요구하게 되었다.

결혼에 대한 이러한 남녀 쌍방간의 암묵적인 계약에도 불구하고 이 계약은 기본적으로 남성에게 유리하고 여성에게 불리한 불공정 계약이자 관행이었다. 결혼 계약을 위반했을 시 가해지는 사회적 제재 및 처벌은 여성에게 훨씬 가혹했다. 특히, 부계 사회의 폐단이라 할 수 있는 축첩제도나 일부다처제가 일상화된 공동체에서는 여성에 대한 차별이 당연시되는 경향마저도 있었다. 특히, 왕이나 권력자 또는 부자들의 축첩은 많은 부작용과 크고 작은 갈등 및 분쟁을 잉태했음에도 불구하고 축첩이 권력과 부를 과시하는 수단으로 이해되면서 현대 사회에서도 부분적으로 유지되고 있다.

21세기 작금에도 아랍-이슬람 사회에서는 공식적으로 일부다처제가 유지되고 있다. 이 제도는 비이슬람 사회가 이슬람 사회를 공격하는 주요 기제이기도 하지만, 이슬람 공동체의 일부다처제는 다른 공동체의 그것과 구분되는 독특한 배경과 특징이 있다.

이슬람 이전 시대 아랍 사회의 결혼제도는 남성 중심의 결혼제도로서 매우 불공정했다. 아랍 사회의 특성상 남성 중심의 사회 풍토가 일찍부터 만들어졌기 때문에 여성과 아내의 지위와 권리는 매우 차별적이며 제한적이었다. 남자는 무제한의 아내를 거느릴 수 있었고, 매매혼, 계약혼, 아내 교환과 임시 동거 등이 아무런 제약없이 이루어졌다.

이슬람의 등장과 함께 여성들에게 일방적으로 불리한 결혼 관행이 개선된 측면이 있다. 꾸란에서는 가정의 의미, 남편과 아내의 역할과 의무, 결혼 혼납금(mahr)의 지급 등 아내의 권리를 보호하기 위한 여러 가지 내용들을 언급하고 있다. 그럼에도 불구하고 꾸란에서 일부다처제를 허용한 것은 무함마드 생존 시에 계속된 전쟁으로 인한 불가피한 측면이 있다.

사도 무함마드에 의해 이슬람교가 만들어지는 과정에서 기성 권력과 무함마드 세력간의 수 많은 전쟁(우후드 전투 등)이 있었고, 이 전쟁으로 인해 많은 남성들이 전사함에 따라 수많은 전쟁 미망인과 전쟁 고아들이 생겨나게 되었다. 정치 지도자로서 무함마드는 이들 미망인과 고아들의 문제에 대한 해결책으로 이들을 인근 가정의 남자들에게 위탁했다. 현대식으로 말하면 국가의 의무를 민간에게 위탁한 것이다.

정치인 무함마드는 이들 미망인과 고아들을 보호하기 위해 이들을 수용한 남자는 이들을 차별하지 못하도록 했다. 즉, 수용된 미망인에게는 정처의 지위를, 고아들에게는 본인의 자식과 똑같은 대우를 하도록 함으로써 차별과 갈등을 없애려 했다. 따라서 4명의 아내까지 허용하는 이슬람 공동체에서 4명의 아내와 그녀들의 자식은 모두 동등한 권리를 가지게 된다. 이와 관련된 꾸란 구절은 다음과 같다.

(꾸란 4장 3절)
"만일 너희가 고아들을 공정하게 대처하여 줄 수 있을 것 같은 두려움이 있다면 좋은 여성과 결혼하라. 두 번 또는 세 번 또는 네 번도 좋으니라. 그러나 그녀들에게 공평을 베풀어 줄 수 없다는 두려움이 있다면 한 여성이거나 너희 오른손이 취한 것과 결혼하라. 그것이 죄를 범하지 않는 가장 좋은 방법이다"

이슬람의 생성 및 확산 시기를 전후로 한 역사적 사실과 상기 꾸란 구절을 통해서 이슬람 사회에서 일부다처제가 허용된 배경은 일종의 사회 복지책의 일환으로 시작되었고 남성들의 성적 욕망과는 무관하다는 것을 알 수 있다. 하지만, 현실 사회에서 일부다처제는 남성들의 욕심과 성적 욕망을 해소하기 위한 수단으로 전락된 경향이 있고 일부다처제에 대한 위의 꾸란 구절은 일부다처제 시행에 대한 종교적·법률적 근거로 악용되는 경향이 있다. 즉, 이는 제도의 문제가 아닌 운용하는 인간들의 문제임을 알 수 있다.

이상에서 살펴본 것처럼, 인간이 선택할 수 있는 유일한 통과의례인 결혼은 결혼 당사자의 사랑과 신뢰를 바탕으로 해야 한다는 원론적인 취지가 무색하게, 시대별, 지역별로 정치·사회·경제·환경·지리적 요소 등이 복합적으로 작용한 제도와 전통이 되어 나름의 형식으로 발전해 왔다. 따라서 결혼 제도는 각 시대별, 지역별 문화적·사회적 특징을 파악할 수 있는 좋은 소재라 할 수 있다.

동지중해 지역은 인류의 4대 문명의 발생지 중 2곳을 포함하고 있는 오리엔트 문명의 발생지다. 따라서 동지중해 지역에서는 초기부터 현대에 이르기까지 결혼 풍습의 다양한 양상과 발전 과정을 한 눈에 볼 수 있는 지역이다.

『동지중해의 결혼 문화와 전통』에서는 인류 문명의 모태를 안고 있는 동지중해에서 변화 및 발달해온 다양한 결혼의 양상을 추적하고 있다. 동지중해는 동양과 서양, 기독교와 이슬람문화가 혼재해 있는 지역이고, 동일 문화권에서도 인종과 민족에 따라 결혼 제도도 차이를 보이고 있다. 또한 인류 문화는 접촉과 교류를 통해 상호 영향을 끼치면서 발달해 왔기 때문에 인간 사회의 대표적인 제도이자 관습인 결혼 역시 상호 영향을 주고 받으며 발전해 왔다.

따라서 본 서에서는 문화교류의 관점에서 동지중해 지역의 다양한 결혼 문화를 보여 주고 있다. 즉, 독자들은 본 서에서 국가, 인종, 민족, 종교와 관습에 따라 구분되는 동지중해 지역의 다양한 결혼 문화와 전통들을 찾아 볼 수 있을 것이다.

1부 '이슬람의 결혼 문화'는 꾸란에 언급된 결혼에 관한 구절을 중심으로 이슬람의 결혼 관행에 대한 설명을 하고 있다. 이슬람교의 인구가 2022년 현재 전 세계 인구의 25%를 차지하고 있고, 5대양 6대주에 널리 분포되어 있지만, 기본적으로 꾸란의 가르침에 절대 복종하는 유일신 종교임을 감안하면 이 글을 통해서 지역을 초월한 이슬람 결혼 관행의 기본 인식, 절차와 구조를 파악할 수 있을 것이다.

2부 '이집트의 결혼 전통과 문화적 다양성'에서는 다른 아랍 국가와 같으면서도 다른 이집트의 결혼 풍속을 볼 수 있을 것이다. 특히, 이집트를 구성하고 있는 무슬림과 기독교 콥트인 그리고 베르베르인들의 결혼 전통 비교를 통해 이집트 문화의 다양성을 즐길 수 있을 것이다.

3부 '요르단의 결혼 문화'에서는 레반트지역 특히 베두인 문화의 특징이 많이 남아 있는 요르단의 결혼 풍속을 볼 수 있을 것이다.

4부 '튀르키예의 결혼 문화'에서는 이슬람 문화를 공유하고 있지만 인종과 민족이 다른 튀르키예 전통 신앙에 기반한 독특한 결혼 풍속을 발견할 수 있을 것이다.

5부 '이란의 결혼 문화'에서는 인종과 민족이 전혀 다르지만 이슬람을 공유하고 있는 그러나 종파가 다른 쉬아(Shia) 이슬람의 종주국인 이란의 결혼 전통을 일견할 수 있을 것이다.

마지막으로 6부 '고대 그리스의 결혼'에서는 동지중해의 가톨릭 문화권을 대표하는 그리스의 결혼 문화와 전통을 이해할 수 있을 것이다. 특히 개인 간 사랑보다 가문 간 계약의 성격이 강했던 고대 그리스의 결혼 문화의 현장을 볼 수 있을 것이다.

문화는 서로 공유되면서 발전하는 속성이 있다. 그 과정에서 기층문화의 특징들이 반영되어 제2, 제3의 변종 문화가 등장하고 궁극적으로 발전적인 방향으로 나아간다는 것을 우리는 경험치를 통해서 알고 있다.

『동지중해의 결혼 문화와 전통』에서는 결혼을 소재로 동지중해 지역의 문화적 상관성을 보여주고 있기 때문에 문화 교류의 관점에서 인류 역사와 문화의 요람인 동지중해의 속살을 파악할 수 있으리라 믿는다.

2022년 여름 남산동 연구실에서
윤 용 수

목차 (Contents)

이슬람의 결혼 문화
(Islamic Marriage Culture)

김수정

(부산외대 아랍학과)

역사의 흐름에 따라 많은 문화와 제도는 변모한다. 그중 결혼은 일관성 있게 그 기조를 유지하고 있는 제도 중 하나이다. 인간은 결혼을 통해 가계(家系)를 이어오고, 부족, 공동체를 유지하며, 국가를 발전시켰다. 결혼을 통해 인간은 자손을 번성시킴으로써, 혈육으로 이루어진 부족을 강화하고, 사회적으로는 사회 구성원을 보충하며 안정을 꾀했다. 이는 곧 인류의 생존과 번영의 가장 기본적인 요건은 바로 결혼이라 할 수 있다. 또한 결혼은 공인된 남녀 두 사람의 결합뿐만 아니라 양가(兩家) 가족의 결합 및 동맹의 성립을 의미한다. 부족주의와 공동체 의식이 강한 아랍 · 이슬람 사회에서의

〈그림1〉 이슬람 결혼

결혼은 이러한 특징이 더욱 강조되었다.

이슬람에서의 결혼은 가계의 존속, 재생산, 가정의 결속과 관계 강화, 사유 재산의 보존, 공동체의 이익을 보호하기 위한 제도인 동시에 인간의 행동을 규제하고 무질서한 성행위로 인한 사회의 혼탁을 예방할 수 있는 제도로 인식되었다(윤용수. 2006:103). 이에 따라 이슬람에서 결혼은 사회적 의무로 여겨지며 남녀의 배우자를 찾는 일은 개인의 일이 아닌 가족 구성원 공동의 일로 간주되었다.

이슬람에서 결혼은 사회적 의무일 뿐만 아니라 종교적 의무이기도 하다. 꾸란(Quran)과 하디스(Hadith)[1]는 인간의 덕목을 유지하기 위해, 종족을 번창시키기 위해, 인간 사이의 사랑과 동정심을 확립하기 위해 결혼 생활을 장려하며 권장하고 있다. 따라서 이슬람의 결혼은 남성과 여성 사이의 신성한 계약이며 영원한 관계에 대한 약속이라 할 수 있다(이희수, 이원삼 외, 2002:102). 이러한 내용은 꾸란에 자세히 언급되어 있다.

> "남성은 여성의 보호자라 이는 하나님께서 여성들보다 강한 힘을 주었기 때문이라 남성은 여성을 그들의 모든 수단으로써 부양하나니 건전한 여성은 헌신적으로 남성을 따를 것이며 남성이 부재시 남편의 명예와 자신의 순결을 보호할 것이라[4:34]."

> "그대 이전에도 하나님은 선지자들을 보내었고 그들에게 배우자를 주어 자손을 갖게 했노라[13:38]."

> "하나님은 너희를 위해 너희 중에서 배우자를 두어 너희 아내들로부터

---

1   이슬람의 예언자인 사도 무함마드의 언행록

아들과 자손을 갖게 하고 너희를 위한 일용할 양식으로는 좋은 것을 주었노라. 그런데 그들이 믿는 것은 헛된 것이니 그들은 하나님의 은혜를 불신함이라[16:72].”

“너희 가운데 독신자를 결혼시켜라[24:32].”

“너희 자신들로부터 배필을 창조하여 그 배필과 함께 살게 하심도 그분 예증의 하나이며 그분은 또한 너희 간에 사랑과 자비를 주셨으니 실로 그 안에는 생각하는 백성을 위한 예증이 있노라[30:21].”

특히 이슬람의 결혼은 남녀 간의 평등을 기초로 한다. 이는 '여성은 남성의 옷이고, 남성은 여성의 옷[2:187]'이라는 꾸란 구절을 통해 남녀 간의 평등 관계가 언급되어 있으며, 이는 무슬림들은 서로의 협력자 및 보호자가 되어 가정 내에서 평등과 상부상조를 통한 관계를 유지해야 함을 의미한다. 실례로 무슬림 여성이 결혼 후 남성 집안의 성을 따르지 않고, 자신의 성을 그대로 사용하는 이유이다.

1. 이슬람의 결혼 과정

이슬람에서의 결혼은 가족 구성원 공동의 일이다. 이슬람 사회를 구성하는 가장 기본 단위는 개인이 아닌 가족 공동체로 여겨지기 때문이다. 각 개인은 자신이 속한 가족 공동체에 대한 연대 의식과 의무, 권리를 갖는다. 이에 따라 결혼을 대상으로 한 남녀는 각자의 배우자를 개인적으로 물색하기보다는 대게 집안의 주선을 통해 물색하거나 그 부모가 자녀의 배우자를 결정한다. 주로 남성의 어머니가 자신의 인맥을 통해 아들에게 적당한 배우자감을 찾는데, 만약 찾지 못할 경우에는 카티바(khatibah)라고 불리는 결혼 중매인을 통해 신부를 물색한다. 카티바의 소개로 신랑은 신붓집을 방문하고, 양측이 서로 마음에들 경우에는 신부 측 집안에 청혼함으로써 결혼 절차가 진행된다. 물론, 신부 측의 거절도 가능하다. 신부 측에서 신랑감이 마음에 들지 않는 경우에는 우회적인 방식으로 거절 의사를 표시한다. 대접한 차나 커피에 소금을 약간 타거나, 간밤의 좋지 않았던 내용의 꿈 이야기, 불길한 징조 이야기를 하는 등 상대방을 배려하며 직설적인 의사를 표하지 않고 우회적으로 거절 의사를 밝힌다.

배우자 결정에는 사회적 의미와 동시에 종교적인 의미도 포함된다. 결혼할 상대자를 아랍어로 나십(nasib)이라 부른다. 이는 운명이라는 뜻으로, 무슬림들은 알라(Allah)가 모든 무슬림들의 배우자를 정해준다고 믿고 있음을 의미한다(엄익란 2007: 128).

이슬람 사회의 결혼 과정은 지역별, 국가별, 가족별로 다르게 나타나지만, 결혼을 위한 협상 및 계약을 결혼의 시작으로 보는 것은 아랍·이슬람 사회의 보편적인 현상이다. 이는 이슬람의 결혼은 알라가 정해준 운명의 배우자를 받아들임과 동시에 양가 가족 간 발생하는 결합 및 약속의 이행으로 여기기 때문이다.

결혼 계약을 위한 합의 과정

이슬람 결혼에서 결혼 계약은 결혼 과정 중 가장 중요한 절차 중 하나이다. 그보다 먼저 결혼 계약서 작성에 앞서 양측 집안은 공식적인 협상 및 합의(ittifaq) 과정을 진행한다. 합의 내용은 집안마다, 지역마다 각기 다르겠지만, 가장 기본적인 내용은 남성은 남편과 아버지의 의무와 권리, 여성은 아내와 어머니의 의무와 권리 이행에 관한 내용과 더불어 결혼 생활 동안 이루어지는 사소한 내용까지도 합의한다는 점이다. 예를 들면 여성의 일할 권리나 학업, 친정집 방문 등이다. 더불어 합의하는 내용은 결혼 시 지급되는 금전, 물품 등에 관한 것들이다. 양측 집안의 가계(家系)를 파악한 후 서로의 상황에 맞게 마흐르(Mahr)[2]의 액수와 물품 내용, 약혼 선물(shabka)의 내용, 신랑의 신혼집 마련, 결혼 비용, 약혼식 비용, 신부가 가져올 혼수의 내용 등을 합의한다. 한쪽 집안의 가세(家勢)가 기울거나 양측이 합의하는 경우는 많은 내용을 생략하고 간단한 예물로 대신하기도 한다.

이슬람의 결혼에서는 대게 신랑 측이 신부 측 보다 큰 비용을 부담한다. 신랑 측이 신혼집을 마련하고, 결혼식 비용을 부담하는 반면, 신부 측은 약혼식 비용과 혼수를 하는 것이 일반적이다. 이러한 내용 모두 합의의 과정에서 논의되는 사항이며, 구체적인 규모나 액수가 거론되는 만큼 민감한 문제로 여겨, 와킬(wakil)이라 부르는 결혼 대리인이 맡아서 진행하기도 한다. 와킬은 주로 친척 중 한 사람이 맡는다. 양가 가족은 합의 과정에서 일어날 수 있는 불협화음을 방지하기 위해 결혼 전 과정을 와킬에게 위임함으로써 원만한 결혼을 성사 시키기 위해 노력한다.

양측의 최종 합의가 완료되면 모든 내용을 작성하고, 그 목록을 신랑과 신부 각각 보관한다. 그 이후 신랑 측이 공식적으로 청혼을 하게 되는데, 이때 청혼하는 사람은 신랑의 아버지, 삼촌, 남자 형제 등 신랑의 남성 가족들이

---

2   결혼시 신랑 측이 신부에게 지불하는 비용이다. 마흐르에 대해서는 다음 장에서 자세히 언급한다.

다. 이후 신부 측에서 청혼을 받아들이면, 정식으로 결혼을 발표하게 된다.

이 과정에서 아버지는 가족의 의견을 대변해주는 역할을 한다면, 신랑, 신부 어머니의 역할은 표면적으로는 드러나지 않지만 보이지 않은 곳에서 많은 영향력을 발휘한다. 신랑, 신부의 어머니는 합의 과정 전에 마흐르의 액수, 혼수 내용 등 결혼에 대한 각종 정보를 사전에 수집하여 합의 과정에 반영되도록 한다.

약혼과 약혼식

이슬람의 결혼에서는 결혼 전 약혼(fatiha)의 절차가 이행된다. 결혼을 양가 가족 간 발생하는 결합 및 계약으로 보는 이슬람에서는 어쩌면 당연한 수순일 것이다. 약혼식은 보통 결혼 신청 합의 후 일주일 이내에 이루어지며, 신붓집에서 거행한다. 이때 신부 측은 손님 접대, 악단, 가수 초대 비용 등을 포함한 모든 비용을 부담한다.

약혼식 때 신랑과 신부 측 결혼 대리인이 서로 손을 잡고 꾸란 제1장인 개경장을 함께 읽는다. 그리고 신부의 결혼 대리인이 "나는 당신에게 나의 딸을 혼인시키겠습니다"라고 말하면 신랑은 "나는 당신 딸과의 혼인을 받아들이며 앞으로 그이를 나의 보호 아래 두겠습니다"라고 대답함으로써 약혼이 성사된다(윤용수. 2006:105).

그리고, 신랑은 신부에게 결혼 협상과 합의 과정에서 논의된 약혼 선물(shabka)을 증정한

〈그림2〉 약혼식

다. 우리나라의 결혼 예물과 같은 것으로, 보통 보석이나 장신구 등이다. 대게 약혼식이나 결혼식에 신부는 이 장신구를 착용하거나, 참석한 손님들에게 자랑하기도 한다.

이러한 절차가 끝나면 약혼 파티를 진행한다. 신부는 드레스(결혼식 때 입을 하얀색 드레스를 제외한)를 입기도 하고, 무용수, 가수 등을 초청하여 성대한 파티를 벌인다. 초대받은 손님들은 신부에게 축하선물이나, 축의금을 주기도 한다.

약혼식이 끝나면 신랑과 신부는 결혼 전까지 서로를 약혼자라 호칭하며 공식적으로 둘의 관계를 인정받고, 자유롭게 양쪽 집안을 왕래한다.

약혼식이 중요한 또 다른 이유는 약혼식을 준비하는 동안, 결혼식 전까지의 약혼 기간 동안에 결혼할 상대방의 가족과 각 집안의 분위기를 익히는 시간이 서로에게 허락되기 때문이다. 이 기간에 한쪽의 중대한 실수, 약점을 발견하거나 상대방이 마음에 들지 않는다면 약혼 취소가 가능하다. 이유가 무엇이던, 신부 측이 약혼 취소를 제안할 경우는 신부는 받은 약혼 선물을 모두 돌려주어야 하며, 신랑 측이 취소할 경우는 선물을 돌려주지 않아도 된다.

결혼 계약과 결혼식

결혼식 날짜는 보통 신랑 측에서 정한다. 신랑 측이 대게 결혼 비용을 부담하기 때문에 신랑 측이 결혼식 비용이 마련되는 것과 신혼집이 완성되는 것을 고려해 날짜를 선택한다. 우리나라처럼 길일(吉日) 같은 것은 없다. 이슬람 국가는 금요일에 집단 예배를 드리므로, 대게 목요일과 금요일이 휴일이다. 이에 따라 많은 커플들이 목요일에 결혼식을 올린다.

한편, 라마단(ramadan) 기간에는 결혼식을 하지 않는다. 그 이유는 라마단

기간에 무슬림들은 해가 떠 있
는 동안, 음료와 음식 섭취를
하지 않을뿐더러 남녀 간 성관
계도 금지되기 때문이다.

결혼식 전 신부와 신부의 친
척들, 친구들은 여성들만을 위
한 밤을 보낸다. 이날을 '헤나

〈그림3〉 헤나의 밤의 헤나 장식

의 밤(laylah al-hanna)라고 부르기도 하는데, 그 이유는 신부 치장을 위해
목욕, 피부마사지, 화장과 함께 신부의 몸에 헤나를 하며 한껏 꾸미기 때문이
다. 헤나는 식물에서 추출한 천연 염색 재료로 아랍 중동 국가의 여성들이 손
과 발을 물들일 때 사용하는 것이다.

여러 가지 치장 방법 중 헤나를 하는 이유는 일부 무슬림들은 헤나가 결혼
을 앞둔 불안한 마음의 신부가 나쁜 진(ginn)[3]에게 노출되어 불행을 당하지
않도록 달래는 데 효험이 있다고 믿었기 때문이다(김정명 외.2005:186). 그
래서 헤나를 하면 행복한 결혼 생활을 할 수 있다는 미신을 믿는다. 헤나를
하는 또 다른 이유는 예쁘게 헤나로 치장하여 결혼식 당일 가장 아름답게 보
이고 싶은 신부의 마음을 드러내며 또한 갓 결혼한 유부녀의 표시를 나타낼
수 있기 때문이다.

이슬람의 전통 결혼식은 신랑집에서 하는 것이 일반적이었다. 그러나 시대
의 변화에 따라 최근에는 전문 결혼식장이나 호텔 등을 빌려서 한다.

결혼 과정에서 가장 중요한 것은 신랑과 신부의 의사 표명과 결혼 계약서

---

3   꾸란에 의하면 천사는 빛으로, 인간은 흙으로, 진은 불로 창조되었다고 명시되어 있다. 진에는 두 종류의
    진이 있는데, 이슬람을 믿는 착한 진(善靈)과 믿지 않는 악한 진(惡靈)이 있다.

〈그림4〉 결혼식 당일

의 서명이다. 이 과정은 마으준(Ma'dhun)이라 불리는 혼인 법무사에 의해
진행되는데, 결혼식 당일 신랑과 신부에게 결혼 의사에 대해 질문하고 신랑
신부는 이에 응답해야만 결혼이 성사된다.

또한 이슬람 결혼에서 합법적인 결혼이 성립되기 위해서는 반드시 결혼
계약서에 서명해야 한다. 이 또한 마으준의 진행하에 이루어진다. 양측 집
안 대표는 결혼 계약서에 서명함으로써 두 집안은 공식적인 관계를 맺게 되
는 것이다.

신랑과 신부 측의 합의 하에 작성된 결혼 계약서에는 신랑과 신부 측 대
표들로 구성된 증인의 서명이 이루어진다. 2명의 남자 증인 또는 1명의 남
자 증인과 2명의 여자 증인으로 구성되며, 대개 신랑이나 신부의 친척들이
나 친구들이 맡는다. 만약 친척이 아닐 경우 증인은 신랑 신부가 결혼하는
사실을 알고, 본인이 증인임을 인지하는 정상적인 사고를 갖춘 무슬림 성인
이어야 한다.

عقد زواج

قال وكيل ـــــــــــــــــــــــــــــ لـ ـــــــــــــــــــــــــــــ :
اسم الزوج   اسم الزوجة

زوجتـك موكلتي ـــــــــــــــــــــــــــــ على كتـاب الله تعالى وسنة
اسم الزوجة

رسوله صلى الله عليه وسلم ، وعلى المــهر المتفق عليه ، وبشهادة الحاضرين والله
خير الشاهدين.

فأجابه ـــــــــــــــــــــــــــــ على الفور:
اسم الزوج

قبلت منك زواجها لنفسي على كتــاب الله تعالى وسنة رسوله صلى الله عليه وسلم ،
وعلى المهر المتفق عليه ، وبشهـادة الحاضرين والله خير الشاهدين.

الساعة ـــــــــــــــ يوم ـــــــــــــــ الموافق ـــــــــــــــــــــــــــــ

المكان ـــ

الشاهد الأول ـــ
الاسم   التوقيع

الشاهد الثاني ـــ
الاسم   التوقيع

الوكيل ـــ
الاسم   التوقيع

الزوجة ـــ
الاسم   التوقيع

الزوج ـــ
الاسم   التوقيع

〈그림5〉 이슬람 결혼 계약서

이때 증인들이 증언을 해야 하는 내용은 신랑과 신부가 이슬람 결혼에서의 금지된 결혼의 관계가 아니라는 점(친남매나 수양 남매 등), 초혼 여부, 양가의 사회적 지위가 비슷한지, 신부가 잇다('idda)기간[4] 중인지 등이다(Antoun. 1972:122).

서명이 끝나면 마으준은 서명된 결혼 계약서를 증거로 결혼 사실을 정부에 등록함으로써, 모든 결혼 절차가 끝난다.

〈그림6〉 계약서 작성

---

4 부부가 이혼을 진행시에 주어지는 이혼숙려기간을 뜻하며, 꾸란에서는 약3개월로 규정하고 있다. 이 기간은 여성이 임신 상태가 아님을 입증하는 기간으로, 만약 여성이 임신했을 때는 출산 전까지 기간이 잇다기간이다.

2. 이슬람 결혼의 특징

이슬람의 결혼제도의 대표적인 특징에는 마흐르(Mahr), 일부다처제, 내혼 (內婚) 및 금지된 결혼제도 등이 있다. 이 중 마흐르와 일부다처제의 경우 남 성의 성적 요구를 충족시키는 매매혼의 수단으로 여기며, 아랍 여성의 인권 을 짓밟는 제도로 간주 되어 많은 비난을 받고 있는 것이 사실이다. 이는 이 슬람의 결혼제도에 대한 무지에 따른 오해라 할 수 있으며, 자세한 내용은 아 래에서 살펴보도록 하겠다.

마흐르(Mahr)[5]

마흐르는 결혼 시에 신랑 측이 신부에게 제공하는 금전적 재화로서, 이슬 람 결혼에 있어 필수 요건이다. 경제적 능력에 따라 마흐르의 제공 범위는 조 정은 가능하나 마흐르 자체를 제공하지 않으면 결혼은 그 법적 효력을 잃기 때문에 반드시 제공해야만 한다.

꾸란에서 결혼을 의미하는 단어는 니카흐(nikah)와 아끄드('aqd)로 나타 난다. 그 단어의 의미는 결합과 계약이다. 이슬람의 결혼은 남성과 여성의 개 인 간 만남을 넘어 양가 가족 간의 결합과 계약을 의미한다. 이에 따라 이슬 람 결혼 과정 중 계약은 꼭 해야만 하는 과정이며, 그 계약 내용 중에 반드시

---

5 많은 서적에서 마흐르를 지참금으로 표기하는 것을 볼 수 있다. 지참금의 사전적 의미는 결혼시 신부 가 신랑에게 제공하는 돈으로서, 이슬람의 마흐르와는 그 결이 다르다. 혹자는 마흐르를 혼납금으로 표현하기도 하지만, 필자는 혼납금이라는 단어의 뜻은 결혼시 지불해야 하는 돈의 의미로 이 단어 또 한 본 제도의 특징을 드러내기에는 역부족이라 여긴다. 이에 따라 필자는 마흐르라는 원어 발음대로 표현하겠다.

포함되어야 하는 사항이 바로 마흐르이다(김수정.2010:37). 마흐르에 대해서는 꾸란과 하디스에 구체적으로 언급하고 있으며, 그 내용은 아래와 같다.

> "결혼할 여자에게 지참금(sadaqah)을 주라 만일 너희에게 그것의 얼마가 되돌아 온다면 기꺼이 수락해도 되니라[4:4]."

> "만일 너희가 그녀들과 동침하지 아니하고 지참금(faridah)을 결정한 후 이혼했다면 결정된 지참금의 절반을 지불 해야 되거늘, 그러나 여성이나 보호자가 용서한다면 제외라 또한 그 용서는 정의에 가장 가까운 것이거늘 양자 사이에 서로가 관대할 것을 잊지 말라[4:25]."

위의 구절을 살펴보면 마흐르는 꾸란에서 '싸다까(sadaqah)'와 '파리다(faridah)'로 언급되고 있다. '싸다까'라는 단어적 의미는 종교적 의무이고, '파리다'라는 단어의 의미는 헌금이다. 이는 마흐르가 남성의 욕구를 충족시키거나, 상업적 거래에 사용되는 수단이 아니라 이슬람의 종교적인 행위이며, 의무임을 명백히 말하고 있다.

마흐르는 현금이거나, 금과 은, 보석류, 가축, 부동산 등 모두 허용된다. 그 범위는 결혼 당사자들 간의 사회적 지위나 경제적 능력에 따라 좌우된다. 이 또한 꾸란에서 언급하고 있다.

> "부유한 자는 부유한 대로 가난한 자는 가난한 대로 자기의 능력에 따라...[2:236]."

위의 꾸란 구절에 언급된 바와 같이 이슬람에서 마흐르의 액수는 신랑 측의 경제적 수준에 따라 부담이 가지 않는 적절한 액수가 권장되고 있다. 대부분의 이슬람 법학자들은 마흐르의 최소 금액과 최대 금액을 규정하지 않았다. 하디스에 따르면 사도 무함마드는 '가장 축복받는 결혼은 최소의 비용으로 가장 간단하게 하는 결혼'이라고 말했다(윤용수. 2006:105).

또한 사도 무함마드는 그의 아내들에게 다양한 액수의 마흐르를 제공했다고 전해진다. 하디스에 언급된 가장 적은 금액의 마흐르는 무쇠로 만든 반지였다. 만약 그조차 줄 수 없는 가난한 남성은 꾸란을 아내에게 가르치는 것으로서 마흐르를 대신하라고 언급하고 있다(조희선. 2009:139). 또한 무함마드는 주인인 남성이 노예 여성을 아내로 맞이할 시 그녀에게 자유를 줌으로써 마흐르를 대신할 수도 있다고 말했다. 이러한 내용을 비추어볼 때 마흐르를 매매혼의 수단으로 보는 일부 시각에는 무리가 있어 보임을 알 수 있다.

한편, 마흐르의 액수와 종류, 지급방식 등은 결혼 합의 과정에서 양측의 협상에 따라 결정된다. 마흐르의 결정은 결혼 합의 과정에서 가장 중요한 일이며, 이에 따라 결혼 대리인인 와킬의 가장 중요한 임무이기도 하다.

마흐르의 결정 이후 재합의를 통해 다시 결정하는 것도 가능하다. 이와 관련하여 꾸란에 언급된 내용은 아래와 같다.

> "지참금이 정해진 이후 상호 합의하여 바꾸어 정해도 너희들에게 죄
> 가 없느니라(4:24)."

마흐르는 아내의 고유의 재산이다. 남편은 마흐르에 대한 어떠한 권리도 가질 수 없다. 결혼 후 마흐르에 대한 사용이나 처분은 오롯이 아내의 권리임이 아래의 꾸란 구절에 명시되어 있다.

"만일 너희가 아내를 다른 아내로 다시 얻으려 할 때 너희가 그녀에게 준 금액 가운데서 조금도 가져 올 수 없노라 너희는 그것을 부정하게 취득하려 하느냐 그것은 분명한 죄악이라(4:20)."

위의 내용에서 알 수 있는 것은 아랍·이슬람 사회에서 마흐르는 부부간 결혼 계약을 지속시키는 역할을 함과 동시에 이슬람 사회에서 비교적 약한 위치에 있는 여성을 보호하기 위한 일종의 사회 보험의 역할을 수행하고 있다는 것이다.

이슬람의 결혼과 이혼 제도는 전통적으로 남성에게 더욱 유리하게 만들어져 있고, 마흐르가 의무화되었던 당시 시대 상황은 전쟁, 질병 등으로 갑작스러운 남성의 사별 등이 빈번했다. 이러한 상황에서 마흐르는 자식들과 혼자 남겨진 여성의 삶을 보장하는 보험의 역할을 한 것이다.

한편, 마흐르에 대한 고전적인 견해는 여성이 결혼함으로써 한 집안에서 다른 집안으로 이동되는 노동력 상실의 대가였다. 그래서 마흐르는 신부 당사자가 아닌, 신부 측 집안에 제공하기도 했다. 물론, 이는 신부의 동의하에서다. 그러나 현재는 아내에 대한 존경과 감사의 표시인 동시에 결혼 기간 또는 그 이후에 아내의 경제적 안정을 위한 것으로 더욱 이해되는 추세임은 분명하다(Richard C. 2004:424).

마흐르의 제공 시점은 결혼 합의 시 결정하고, 계약서에 그 내용을 명시한다. 마흐르는 결혼 계약일에 제공하기도 하고, 결혼식 당일에 제공하기도 한다. 또는 양측이 협의한 다른 날을 정해서 제공하기도 한다. 드문 예이나, 결혼 시에는 상징적인 약간의 액수만 지급하고, 남성의 사망 또는 이혼 시에 남은 차액을 제공하기도 한다. 이런 제공 방식의 목적은 부부간 이혼을 방지하고, 이혼 후 여성의 생계를 보호하기 위한 방법이었다(Hedaya Hartford & Ashraf Muneeb. 2001:16).

일부다처제

많은 이들에게 일부다처제는 이슬람의 결혼에만 존재하는 제도라 여겨지고 있다. 그러나 이 제도는 동서양을 막론하고 고대부터 전 세계에 널리 행해지던 결혼풍습이었다. 민주주의의 발현지라 여겨지는 고대 그리스 시대는 물론이며, 로마, 비잔틴 제국 시대, 페르시아의 결혼제도에도 일부다처제를 발견할 수 있다. 또한 구약과 신약성경에 등장하는 다수의 선지자의 아내도 여러 명이었다는 것은 부인할 수 없는 사실이다. 유대인들의 결혼풍습에도 일부다처제가 한 특징으로 나타난다. 그리하여 유대교의 정신적 지주의 역할을 한다고 전해지는 탈무드에는 랍비들은 많은 수의 아내를 거느리는 유대인들의 결혼 관습에 대해 아내를 4명만 두는 것으로 제한한 사례도 있다 (김정명 외. 2005:192).

일부다처제가 이슬람 결혼제도의 특징으로 정착한 배경은 예언자 무함마드 시대의 역사 속에서 찾을 수 있다. 예언자 무함마드가 이슬람 공동체를 결성한 이후 625CE년에 메카의 꾸라이쉬(Quraish) 부족과 메디나의 무슬림들 간에 우후드(Uhud)전투가 발생했다. 이 전투에서 무슬림은 참배를 맞이했고, 이로 인해 무슬림 내에서 많은 미망인과 고아들이 발생했다. 이들을 구제하기 위한 한 방법으로 일부다처제가 등장했으며, 이는 전쟁이나 질병으로 발생한 미망인들을 구제하기 위한 사회보장책 차원에서 시행되었다.

또한, 일부 학자들은 일부다처제를 부부간 성적(性的)인 부분과 출산에 문제가 생겼을 시에 유용한 해결책이 될 것이라 보기도 한다(김정명 외. 2005:193). 아내가 정신적, 육체적 장애가 있을 때는 이혼을 하기보다 오히려 새로운 아내를 둠으로써 부부 관계를 지속해 나가는 것이 합리적인 해결책이라 보고 있으며, 부부간 아이가 생기지 않았을 경우 또한 일부다처제를 통하는 편이

더 현명하다는 견해다.

그러나 어떤 이유를 막론하고 아내의 수를 무제한 적으로 허용하지는 않는다. 이슬람에서 허용하는 부인의 수는 4명이며 이 또한 모든 부인에게 정신적, 육체적, 경제적으로 동등하게 대우해야 한다는 조건 아래에서만 가능하다. 만약 여러 명의 부인에게 동등하게 대우할 수 없는 상황이라면 첫 번째 부인을 제외한 새로운 여성과 결혼할 수 없다.

즉 남성이 여러 명의 아내를 둔다면 모든 부인은 동등한 대우와 권리를 공평하게 가질 수 있으며, 또한 남편의 사망 시 아내들은 모두 같은 수준의 유산을 받고, 자식들도 같은 서열에 위치한다. 꾸란에 언급된 일부다처제에 관한 내용은 다음과 같다.

> "만일 너희가 고아들을 공정하게 대하여 줄 수 없을 것이라고 염려가 된다면 너에게 좋다고 여겨지는 여성과 결혼하라. 둘 또는 셋 또는 네 명도 좋으니라. 그러나 아내들을 공정하게 대해 줄 수 없을 것 같은 염려가 있다면 한 명의 여성과 결혼하라[4:3]."

> "너희가 최선을 다한다고 하여 아내들을 공평하게 할 수 없으리라. 한 쪽으로 치우쳐 매달린 여인처럼 만들지 말라 만일 너희가 화해하고 알라를 공경한다면 하나님으로부터 관용과 자비가 있을 것이라[4:129]."

위의 꾸란 구절에서 살펴본 바와 같이 꾸란에서는 원칙적으로는 일부일처제를 권장하고 있으나, 일부다처제를 시행할 경우에는 반드시 남성이 모든 부인에게 공평한 대우를 해야만 가능하다는 것을 알 수 있다.

한편 두 번째 부인을 두는 상황이라면, 반드시 첫 번째 부인의 동의를 구해야 한다. 다음 차 수의 부인도 마찬가지이다. 즉 첫 번째 부인의 동의가 없

고, 남편이 모두 동등하게 대우할 수 없다면 일부다처제는 시행할 수 없는
것이다.

내혼(內婚)과 금지된 결혼

'최고의 배우자는 사촌'이라는 말이 있다. 유목민 사회였던 아랍 · 이슬람
사회는 전통적으로 내혼을 권장해왔다. 그 이유는 부족주의와 공동체 의식
이 강한 아랍 사회에서 결혼은 개인 간의 결합의 의미를 넘어 공동체를 강화
하고, 부족의 존속 및 강화의 수단이었기 때문이다. 그로 인해 혈연관계를 더
욱 강화하고, 공동체의 목적과 이익 추구를 위해 사촌 간 결혼하는 내혼 풍습
이 발생하게 되었다. 즉, 내혼을 통해 부족 간 결혼을 통해 순수한 혈통을 유
지하며, 내부 결속력을 강화하려는 목적인 셈이다.

내혼 중에서도 부계 혈통의 결혼이 주를 이룬다. 결혼 대상은 사촌, 친인척
이며 뿐만 아니라, 소속되어 있는 같은 공동체, 같은 종교 분파 등의 구성원
이다. 부족 내 구성원 한 명은 노동력 하나로 인식되었던 사회였기 때문에 내
혼을 한다면 결혼으로 발생하는 노동력 상실을 방지할 수 있고, 금전적 재화
의 손실도 막을 수 있다. 왜냐하면 결혼 시 제공해야 하는 마흐르가 다른 부
족으로 가는 이탈을 막을 수 있기 때문이다. 또 다른 장점은 내혼을 할 경우
다른 부족과의 결합, 동맹으로 인한 가족의 분리 아닌, 한 부족 내에 남성과
여성이 둘 다 머무르게 되므로 분쟁의 발생 요소도 적다는 점이다.

내혼 풍습은 비단 이슬람 결혼제도에만 존재하는 것이 아니다. 고대 페르
시아, 바빌로니아, 고대 이집트 등 빈번히 시행되던 제도였다. 지배 계층들
의 남매간 결혼을 통해 왕족의 순수혈통 유지와 재산 이탈 방지를 위해 내혼
을 전략적으로 이용했던 것이다. 고대의 특권층만의 전유물이었던 내혼 풍

습은 점차 확산되었고, 이슬람의 출현과 더불어 모든 계층에 전파되었다(김정명 외. 2005.178).

앞서 언급한 이유로 이슬람에서는 내혼을 가장 이상적인 결혼의 형태로 보고 이를 권장한다. 그렇지만 모든 친인척과 결혼을 할 수 있는 것은 아니다. 이슬람에서는 그 대상을 사촌 이상으로 제한하고 있으며, 남성과 여성 사이에 가까운 근친 관계가 성립되는 경우 마흐람(mahram, 금혼 대상)이 된다. 이와 관련된 꾸란에 언급된 내용은 아래와 같다.

> "너희 아버지들이 결혼한 여자들과 결혼하지 말라 과거에 지나간 것은 제외되나 그것은 수치요 증오이며 저주받은 관습이라(4:22)."

위의 구절에서 알 수 있는 내용은 남성의 경우 자신의 아버지와 혼인 관계에 있었던 여인들과의 결혼은 금지된다. 즉, 아버지의 이혼 한 부인이나 아버지의 사망으로 미망인이 된 계모 등이다. 이슬람 이전 시대는 정형화된 결혼제도의 부재(不在)와 비윤리적이고 비도덕적인 제도의 형태가 만연한 사회였다. 이슬람 이전에는 가능했던 결혼의 형태가 이슬람의 출현 이후 금지된 것이다.

또한 어머니와 여동생, 딸 등 가까운 친족관계의 결혼을 금지하고 있으며, 그 내용은 아래와 같다.

> "너희들에게 금지된 것이 있으니 어머니들과 딸들과 누이들과 고모들과 외숙모들과 형제의 딸들과 누이의 딸들과 너희를 길러준 유모들과 같은 젖을 먹고 자란 양녀들과 아내들의 어머니들과 너희 부인들이 데려와 너희의 보호를 받는 의붓딸들이라. 너희가 아직 그녀들과 부부생활을 하지 아니했다면 너희가 그들의 딸들과 결혼해도 죄악이 아니나 너희 아들

들의 아내들과 결혼은 금지라. 또한 너희가 두 자매를 동시에 부인으로
맞아도 아니 되나 지나간 것은 예외라[4:23]."

위 내용을 살펴보면 결혼 금지 대상은 친어머니, 할머니, 유모, 딸, 손녀, 여자
형제, 고모, 이모, 외숙모, 남자 형제 측 조카, 여자 형제 측 조카 등이다. 이러
한 결혼 금지 대상을 둔 이유는 아주 가까운 근친 간 결혼의 경우 그 부부의
자녀가 유전적으로 신체적, 정신적 결함의 발생 확률이 크기 때문이라 보기
때문이다. 또한, 샤리아(Sharia)[6]에서는 가까운 친척관계에서의 사랑은 자연
스럽게 발생하기 때문에 가까운 친인척 간의 성적 관계를 금한다고 언급하
고 있다(황의갑. 2008:105).

또한 유모, 같은 젖을 먹고 자란 양녀, 장모, 의붓딸, 며느리, 동시에 두 자
매를 결혼 대상으로 삼는 것도 금지다. 같은 혈육은 아니지만, 어머니 같은
존재나 같은 젖을 통한 형제자매 등은 가까운 친인척으로 보았기 때문이다.
그리고 유부녀와의 결혼도 금지된다. 만약 이미 결혼한 여성이 이혼하는 경
우나 전남편이 사망할 경우는 결혼할 수 있다. 이혼녀일 경우는 임신 가능성
을 위해 3개월의 유예기간이 지난 후 결혼할 수 있으며, 전남편이 죽은 경우
는 4개월 10일의 애도 기간이 지난 후에 재혼할 수 있다.

"이미 결혼한 여성과도 금지되나...[4:24]."

"이혼한 여성은 삼 개월을 기다리게 되나니...[2:228]."

---

6   이슬람교의 종교 율법으로, 종교적인 내용뿐만 아니라 가족생활, 사회생활 등 무슬림들의 모든 일상생
    활을 지도하고, 따르는 생활 규범이다.

"남편이 죽어 과부를 남길 때 그 과부는 사 개월 십 일을 기다려야 하
노라(2:234)."

위와 같이 꾸란에 언급된 금지의 내용은 이슬람 이전 시대의 잘못된 결혼
제도를 재정비함으로써 이슬람의 결혼제도 체계를 갖추어나간 이슬람의 노
력으로 비친다.

이슬람에서는 신앙이 없는 여성이나 유일신교도 이외의 우상 숭배자와의
결혼 또한 금지하고 있다. 이는 같은 무슬림들끼리 결혼 함으로써 이슬람 공
동체의 분열 및 파괴를 막고자 하는 방책이다. 꾸란에 언급된 내용을 다음
과 같다.

"믿음이 없는 여성과 결혼하지 말라 믿음을 가진 여자 노예가 믿음
이 없는 유혹하는 매혹의 여자보다 나으니라. 또한 믿음이 없는 남성들
이 믿음을 가질 때까지 딸들을 결혼시키지 말라. 믿음을 가진 노예가 믿
음이 없는 유혹하는 매혹의 남성보다 나으니라. 이들은 지옥으로 유혹하
도다(2:221)."

"너희 가운데 부유하고 신앙이 두터운 여성과 결혼할 수 없는 자는 너
희들의 오른손이 소유한 자들 가운데서 신앙심이 두터운 하녀들과 결혼
함이 나으니라(4:25)."

이슬람에서는 무슬림 간의 결혼을 가장 이상적인 결혼 형태로 보고 있으
며 이를 권장한다. 그러나 결혼 대상 중 무슬림이 없는 경우는 남성은 기독
교인이나 유대교인 등 유일신을 믿는 종교인 여성들과의 결혼은 가능하다고
언급한다. 이슬람에서는 기독교와 유대인의 경우 성서의 백성(people of the

book)으로 부르며 같은 유일신을 믿는 것으로 여기기 때문이다. 그러나 반대로 여성은 불가하다. 부계 중심 사회인 이슬람 사회에서 무슬림 여성과 다른 종교인 남성의 결혼은 이슬람 공동체의 분열로 이어질 수 있기 때문으로 보기 때문이다. 한편, 무신론자들과는 결혼은 모두 금지된다.

> "그대 이전에 성서를 받은 자들의 여성들도 너희가 그녀들에게 마흐르를 지불하고 그들과 화목하게 살 때는 허락된 것이거늘 간음을 해서도 안 되며 내연의 처를 두어서도 아니 되나니(5:6]."

또한, 간통을 저지른 사람은 무신론자 및 간통을 저지른 사람과의 결혼만 허락된다. 즉 간통을 저지른 자 그리고 매춘부의 결혼은 금지되어 있음을 알 수 있으며, 이는 아래의 꾸란 구절에서 확인할 수 있다.

> "간통한 남자는 간통한 여자 또는 신을 믿지 아니한 여자 외에는 결혼할 수 없으며 간통한 여자는 간통한 남자 또는 신을 믿지 아니한 남자 외에는 결혼할 수 없나니 이것은 믿는 신도들에게 금지되어 있노라 (24:3]."

이처럼 이슬람의 결혼은 내혼을 통한 혈통의 강화와 재산권 보호, 통치 권력 강화 등을 목적으로 시행되었지만, 그 결혼 대상의 일부를 제한함으로써 종교적, 사회적인 문제를 방지했음을 알 수 있다.

'무지의 시대'라 불리는 이슬람 이전 시대의 결혼은 비도덕적, 비윤리적이며 남성 중심의 형태가 많았다. 그러나 이슬람의 출현으로 인간이 집단 속에서 지켜야 할 다양한 보편적 규범과 질서, 관행, 평등 등이 동시에 나타났다.

이에 따라 이슬람의 결혼제도 또한 많은 변화가 일어났다.

이슬람은 유일신을 믿고, 그에 복종할 것을 가르치는 종교다. 무슬림들은 꾸란과 샤리아에 언급된 종교적 교리에 순응하며 살아가며, 과거부터 현재까지 충실히 지켜오고 있다. 무슬림들은 결혼은 유일신 하나님이 인간에게 하사한 축복 중의 하나라 여기며, 신성한 종교적 의무이자 사회적 필연성이라 여긴다.

이슬람의 다양한 결혼제도가 발생한 배경과 이유, 현재까지 지속되는 역사적, 사회적, 종교적 환경에 대한 이해가 필요한 시점이라 하겠다.

참고문헌

김수정. 2010.『동지중해권의 결혼 지참금 연구-고대 그리스, 로마, 아랍 이슬람 사회를 중심으로』.
　　　부산외국어대학교 석사 학위 논문.
김정명 외. 2005.『세계의 혼인문화』. 한국외국어대학교 외국학종합연구센터.
윤용수. 2006. 이슬람의 결혼 관행.『한국이슬람학회논총』. 한국이슬람학회. pp.101-120.
이희수. 이원삼 외. 2002.『이슬람』. 파주: 청아출판사.
엄익란. 2007.『이슬람의 결혼 문화와 젠더』. 한울 아카데미.
조희선. 2009.『이슬람 여성의 이해: 오해와 편견을 넘어서』. 서울: 세창출판사.
최영길. 2001. 성 꾸란 의미의 한국어 번역. 파하드 국왕 성 꾸란 출판청.
황의갑. 2008. 무슬림의 결혼에서의 허용과 금지.『국제문화연구』. 국제문화연구원. pp.101-119.
Antoun, Richard T. 1972. *Arab Village: A Social Structural Study of a Trans-Jordanian Peasant Community*. Bloomington and London: India University.
Hartford Hedaya & Ashraf Muneeb. 2001. *Your Islamic Marriage Contact*. Dar Al Fikr.
Richard C. Martin. 2004. *Encyclopedia of Islam and the Muslim world*. Thomson Gale.

사진 출처

〈그림 1〉 https://www.freepik.com/free-photo/young-muslim-bride-groom-wedding-photos_1
　　　4378163.htm#query=arab%20marrige&position=4&from_view=search&track=ais
〈그림 2〉 https://www.almrsal.com/post/1132799?utm_source=google.com&utm_medium=or
　　　ganic&utm_campaign=google.com&utm_referrer=google.com%3E
〈그림 3〉 https://arabi21.com/Content/Upload/large/1120172518204147.jpg
〈그림 4〉 https://3.bp.blogspot.com/-BqKaw1uiBO8/VG_U1-AXryI/AAAAAAAAOU0/sE5o
　　　CW3WWi4/s1600/1551779_372935912864568_4344395852151242005_n.jpg
〈그림 6〉 https://mawdoo3.com/

2부

이집트의 결혼 전통과 문화적 다양성
(Marriage Traditions and Cultural Diversity in Egypt)

모나 파루끄(Mona Farouk M. Ahmed)
(부산외대 지중해지역원)

I. Introduction

Egypt is a country with a long history and a great ancient civilization. Throughout its ancient history, Egypt extended its territories to include many people of different origins and cultures. Also, Egypt has invited foreigners to settle in its lands with its strategic location in the middle of the world linking Asia, Europe, and Africa through the Red Sea, and the Mediterranean Sea, which are connected through the Egyptian waterway of the Suez Canal. Unfortunately, all those merits attracted foreign colonialism to Egypt with its richness of both natural and human resources. Thus, many foreigners settled in Egypt during those periods of different colonialism including Turkish, French, and British occupation which was the last one that extended for more than 70 years till the mid of the twentieth century. The result of all this foreign influence was a society of multicultural diversity in Egypt.

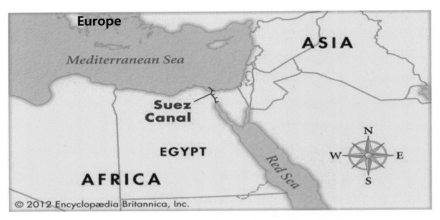

〈Figure 1〉 The Strategic Location of Egypt Linking the Three Old Continents

In this chapter, we will explore this diversity through the traditions of marriage in different parts of Egypt. After giving an overview of the marriage concept in Egyptian society, we will start with Cairo, the capital of Egypt, introducing the different marriage traditions in this city where a majority of Muslims live with a minority of Christian Copts. Thus, we can explore the differences in the marriage traditions between Egyptian Muslims and Copts, which can give us a general trend of Egyptian marriage traditions at the present. Then, we will introduce some other distinctive marriage traditions of other groups living in Egypt, including Bedouins of Siwa oasis who live in the north west of Egypt, and Nubians who live in the south of Egypt.

II. The marriage concept in Egyptian Society

I. Factors influencing marriage in Egypt

The marriage concept in Egypt is related to religion as Egyptian society consisted of a Muslim majority with a Christian minority. Marriage according to both Islam and Christianity is a holy tie with a religious commitment. Muslims call marriage "the half of the religion"[1] as it is the cornerstone on which communities grow. Accordingly, the religion whether Islam or Christianity is reflected in most of the marriage traditions and matters starting with the wedding ceremony held in worship places of Mosques and churches, and ending with all legal regulation concerning marriage or divorce which is based on the religious laws for both Muslims and Christians.[2] In addition to religion, there are many factors reflect the matters of marriage including the educational and economic backgrounds of the families.

---

1   Among the Hadiths of Prophet Mohammad confirming the importance of marriage: Anas ibn Malik reported: The Messenger of Allah, peace, and blessings be upon him, said, "Whoever Allah provides with a righteous wife, Allah has assisted him in half of his religion. Let him fear Allah regarding the second half." (Source: al-Mu'jam al-Awsat 992)

2   The Egyptian personal status law, which is related to marriage and divorce, is based on the Islamic law (sharî'a) with the dominant view of the Hanafi school of the Muslim Sunnite schools of law as it was the official school of the Ottoman Empire ruled Egypt for so long. As for Christians in Egypt, they maintain their religious legislation regarding marriage and divorce according to the laws of their religion (Bernard-Maugiron 2010, 3, 25).

Living in big cities, or in the countryside, also had its impact on the marriage traditions in Egypt. There are also special communities in Egypt preserving their own traditions which can be seen clearly in their marriage traditions. Among those communities, Bedouins and Nubians are good examples. Most of those communities try to maintain their identity by arranging marriages within their communities. This resulted in the increase in consanguineous marriage in Egypt, especially in the rural areas. For people of other countries like South Korea, it may be strange to know that there are many cases of marriages between first cousins in Egypt. This is legally allowed as it is not prohibited by Muslims or by Copts who are the main Christian sects in Egypt. Among other Egyptian Christians, the Egyptian Catholic Church prohibits marriage among cousins (Allam 2019).

In brief, we can say that many factors influence the marriage decision in Egypt. Among those factors, religion, urbanization, economic status, and Education have a strong influence, similar to other societies in the Middle East.

2. Trends of Marriage in Egypt

Statistics of Marriages in Egypt showed the continuous high rate of consanguineous marriages despite the expectations that it would decline due to the modernization process. In this context, some data stated that consanguineous marriages continued steadily to comprise about a quarter of the total marriages in Egypt, precisely 23% of the total marriages of 1965, declining only to 21% in 2000. Among those consanguineous marriages, the most common was for marriage to the father's brother's son, and father's sister's son with a stronger trend among the people with less education (El-Tawila and Khadr 2004, 52). Some factors behind the increase of consanguineous marriages in Egypt are seen in seeking to keep the properties within the one family through those marriages. Also, the economic factor can be seen as one of those factors, as some data showed that marriage costs "half price" if it was among relatives. Especially, seeing that the housing cost can be one of the main obstacles to marriage among Egyptian young people, while it is almost lower than half of the cost when living with relatives (Singerman 2008, 15).

As for the average age of marriage in Egypt, the official statistics declared by the Egyptian Central Agency for Public Mobilization and Statistics showed that the age of marriage among males on average was 30.4 years, compared to 24.7 years among females in 2020. Cairo, the capital of Egypt with the largest population among the Egyptian cities, recorded the highest average age of marriage for males and females in Egypt with about 32.9 years and 28.6 years, respectively. The lowest average age was in rural areas of Egypt in

Upper Egypt and the Nile Delta (Mamdouh 2021). Despite increasing the age of marriage through Egypt's Child Law to 18 years old for girls since 2008, Egypt's Demographic Surveys showed that many Egyptian girls under 18 continued to get married, as the statistical data showed a steady trend in the percentage of women aged 20 to 24 years who were married before the age of 18 from 2005 to 2008 with about 16% and ironically it increased slightly to 17.4% in 2014. Moreover, there is still a percentage of women married before the age of 15 is recorded though with a declining trend from 3.9% in 2000 to 2.0 % in 2014. The median age of the first marriage among Egyptian women also showed low age of 20.8 years. The education level influences these rates, as the age of marriage is higher among educated women (UNICEF 2017, 5, 6). However, in general, we can note that early marriage is widely spread in Egypt especially in rural areas and among low-educated people.

This was a quick overview of the marriage situation in Egypt before we explore the variety of marriage traditions that we can find in Egyptian society rich with diverse cultures.

3. Costs of marriage in Egypt

One of the main barriers to marriage in Egypt would be the high cost. This is related to religious obligations of marriage giving responsibilities over men to cover most of the costs of marriage.

According to Islamic traditions, men are responsible for preparing the house and for paying a dowry, called "mahr" in Arabic, for the future wife before marriage. The amount of mahr is decided matching the social and economic standards of the families. This is simply what is about the cost of marriage according to Islamic teachings which also recommend not to exaggerate the amount of mahr or the specifications of the house and to facilitate the marriage for people.

Despite these religious teachings, the real expenses required for marriage in Egypt are highly exaggerated to add other costs including a golden or diamond present called "Shabka", and insisting on providing a large house fully equipped with all kinds of household appliances and luxurious furniture for several rooms, including the guest room, the dining room and room for the future children. Of course, these requirements differ based on the economic and social level of families, but generally Egyptian families compete in requiring better standards of life for the future life of their children when they are preparing for marriage, so they exaggerate in their conditions about the marital house.[3]

Egyptians even exaggerate weddings to look as luxurious as they can. This all resulted in heavy expenditures for marriage in Egypt.

---

3   This is based on the eyewitness of the author of this chapter according to her experience as an Egyptian lived in the Egyptian society for long enough to directly examine those facts.

Actually, the celebrations related to marriage are not only weddings, as there is an engagement party and before the engagement, there is also a "Fatiha" meeting between the families reading the opening verses of the Quran as a sign of agreement about the marriage. Also, Henna parties and parties for signing the marriage contract called in Arabic "Katb El-Kitab" are introductory celebrations for the final weddings. Usually, luxurious weddings have long programs that last for the whole night in luxurious hotels with luxurious dinners.

There was a study conducted in 1999 on 105 Egyptian families in Egypt showed that the average total marriage cost was 20,194 L.E. (5,957$), which exceeds the Egyptian GNP per capita by more than four times. More surprisingly, that study stated that even those who live below the poverty line in Egypt had spent 9,466 L.E. on marriage costs, as those poor families usually indebt themselves for covering marriage costs for their children (Singerman 2008, 9, 12). The same study also noted that the size of newlywed houses is getting larger over time, as it required furnishing only one room for couples married in 1965, increased to three rooms in 2000. Actually, the housing costs in Egypt absorb about a third of marriage costs while furnishing the houses costs about 28% of the costs of marriage. In Egypt, the furniture of a house evaluates the status of the couple reflecting the economic and financial status of their families.

Thus, usually buying the furniture includes negotiations between the families of the couple before marriage concerning its required quality, quantity, and models, which sometimes leads to disputes among those families over this issue (Singerman 2008, 13).

Ironically, there is a special job for organizing the newlywed house, and some YouTubers do this job and make videos of those Egyptian newlywed houses. Surprisingly, some of those houses in the rural areas of Egypt showed crazy numbers of hundreds of bedcovers and towels while organizing bedrooms. The house organizer was explaining this as Egyptian traditions for families competing to show their best while furnishing their children's newlywed houses. Some comments for those YouTube videos were by people of other Arab countries who were shocked by those numbers and wondered what to do with all of those towels or whether they will be inherited through generations. This is just an example of the exaggeration of marriage costs in Egypt.

Ⅲ. Customs and traditions of Marriage in Egypt

In this part, we will explore the variety of marriage traditions in different areas of Egypt to feel the richness of cultural diversity enjoyed by Egyptian society. We will start with the Egyptian capital,

Cairo, to see the main trend of marriage traditions in modern Egypt. Then, we will see other traditions preserved by some distinctive groups of Egyptian society like Amazigh of Siwa, Nubians of Aswan, and the Bedouins of Sinai.

1. Cairo

Being the capital and the largest populated city in Egypt make Cairo a representative city of the mainstream trends of Egyptian culture. The Cairenes, people of Cairo, consist of different origins but are mainly dominant by a majority of Egyptian Muslims and a minority of Egyptian Christians. Many of those Cairenes were originally born in other cities and then moved to the capital for better education and career. As I am a Cairene, I will introduce the Cairene culture and traditions related to marriage through my experience and eyewitnesses.

Usually, the costs of marriage are divided between the man and woman who decided to get married while their families financially support them. Men should provide the house and pay the dowry (mahr) to the pride. In turn, the women use this mahr in furnishing the house, which usually costs double the amount of that mahr. The man also is responsible for buying all electrical appliances like the refrigerator, washing machine, and Television. Some families see no value in receiving mahr as they will pay more for furniture so they choose to share the cost of the furniture between the couple instead of receiving mahr. Thus, if the house consists of 4 rooms (Bedroom, guest room, living room, dining room), which is common in Cairo, each one of the couple should furnish 2 rooms. The Kitchen cabinets and the bathroom components are provided by the groom, while the Kitchen tools and utensils are provided by the bride according to the traditions. This is usually the concept of dividing the marriage costs between the couples. Of course, there are exceptions like marriage among celebrities with cases where the rich side covers all the marriage expenses unconditionally.

As for the golden or diamond presents called "Shabka", which the groom should give to the bride, its cost is decided according to the social and economic level standards of their families. It basically consists of two couple rings called "Diblah" through which people can distinguish between engaged or married people and non-married people, as this simple ring (see Fig. 2) has to be always worn in the right hand of the engaged person whether man or woman and then it is moved to the left hand after their marriage distinguishing them from single people. It is really not acceptable to take off that ring once you wear it because if you are engaged or married while you don't wear that ring you will be suspected of the bad intention of pretending to be single. The names of the couple and the date of their engagement are written inside each of these couple rings, which symbolize their commitments from that date.

〈Figure 2〉 The shape of Diblah (Couple rings)

Besides the couple rings, men should give that jewelry present of Shabka for the pride, usually Gold (18K or 21K) or Diamond. The average prices of Shabka range between 20,000 to 100,000 L.E. as reported in a news article in 2019 (El-Shamma 2019).

The celebrations of marriage in Cairo differ not only according to the economic and social level of the couples but also their education and ideological background have an influence on their decisions concerning those celebrations. For example, some independent couples choose to save these expenses and rather spend them for a honeymoon trip or other essential needs of their newly established family. For some others, they compete to commemorate those events through unique celebrations regardless of the costs.

The usual pattern of those celebrations is that both families of the groom and the bride give their conditions of the number of guests who should be invited from their relatives and friends on an equal basis among the two families. They also negotiate about the proper place for holding those celebrations. The main celebrations are the engagement party and the wedding party. The common tradition is that the cost of the engagement party is paid by the family of the bride while the wedding cost is paid by the groom's family. Sometimes, the two families decide to share equally the expenses for both parties.

As for the Fateha meeting, it is a close meeting in the house of the bride basically with only the two families while sometimes some relatives or close friends are invited. As reading the Fateha verses of the Quran takes only a few seconds, this meeting often is done occasionally when the groom's family visits the bride's family to receive their acceptance of the marriage proposal. The henna party is also prepared by the bride in her family's house inviting only girls and women of the family and friends. Thus, the costs of this event are covered by the bride's family. This henna ceremony was traditionally common in rural areas of Egypt in the past, but with the international appreciation of henna decorations and with the increase of modern fashions based on traditional concepts, the henna ceremonies started to increase in Cairo and among people of high class paying for henna experts to prepare special programs in those henna parties usually took place in the day before the wedding.

I remember that when I got married in 1999, I did not have to think about the henna party as it was only common in rural areas by that time. But when my friend got married later in 2004, she invited me to her henna party held at her house where many women and girls gathered with a henna designer who drew henna for the bride and the invitees. Also, the henna designer provided the bride with several dresses with different themes for a variety of dancing the bride performed as a part of the program of this henna event, which became common and fashionable for people of Cairo till now.

Modernity and westernization had their impacts, as there are in-creasing cases of couples already dating for quite long before tak-ing the marriage decision so they would escape the Fateha meeting and some even escape the engagement part and suddenly inform people of their wedding date. This case usually can be seen among celebrities. Also, although traditionally the wedding is celebrated in the evening and lasts until midnight or even longer, some couples adopt the western style of celebrating their wedding in the daylight in open places which was not common in Egyptian society in the past. Actually, in the past as at least till the 1960s and 70s those parties were simple and usually held inside the families' houses but gradually with increasing the invitees and seeking to look more luxurious, wedding halls of hotels were the proper places to hold those celebrations competing with luxurious programs that some-times include singers and dancers of celebrities adding crazy costs for those events.

The marriage celebrations of the Copts are similar to those of Muslims for the engagement and wedding parties. The difference is that Copts do not have Fateha meetings as they of course do not have to read Quran. Also, Muslims have another celebration for signing the Islamic marriage contract called "Katb Al-Kitab", which usually is held in mosques or Islamic institutions. Instead of that, Copts have their religious ceremony held in the churches which usually takes place right before the wedding, as it often takes only 45 minutes of rituals including scripture readings, crowning

〈Figure 3〉 Ritual ceremonies for Copts in Cairo

the bride and groom with special crowns and gowns, and the priest anointing them with holy oil on their forehead for blessings and spiritual protection as seen in the picture (Fig. 3) showing the couples wearing the crowns and special gowns.

Those ceremonies of Cairene whether Muslims or Christians are similar to other Egyptian cities as it represents the common trend for the marriage traditions in Egypt. Special traditions can be found for special groups like Bedouins, Nubians, and Amazigh of Egypt, which will be introduced in the following parts.

2. Siwa

⟨Figure 4⟩ Egypt's map Siwa oasis

Siwa is an Egyptian oasis located in Matrouh governorate near the Libyan borders (as seen on the map in Fig. 4). This oasis is distinctive with its Berber inhabitants, who are called also the Amazigh of Egypt. They maintain their special traditions and cultural heritage, which can be seen in their continuing living in traditional mud-brick houses that appeared like caves (seen in Fig. 5). Siwa Oasis is famous for its fertile lands producing good quality of dates and olives that are widely exported

(The Editors of Encyclopaedia. 2016).

〈Figure 5〉 Traditional Houses of Mudbricks in Siwa Oasis

The people of Siwa (Siwans), like other Amazigh, still live in other African countries like Libya, Tunisia, Algeria, and Morocco, are an indigenous North African group that has their language called "Tamazight" with their Siwan dialect. In Egypt, the Siwans are not pure Amazigh as they are mixed with other Sudanese and Bedouin races (Hammad 2009, 769). Their living in Siwa oasis with its relatively isolated location in the desert helped them to maintain their language and nomadic traditions. The majority of Siwan people, who are about 20 thousand people, are Muslims like other Egyptians, but many still preserve pre-Islamic customs based on their traditions (Abdou

2022). They belong to 11 tribes preserving their tribal rules and each tribe has a leader called "Sheikh of the tribe". Their life mainly depends on palms and olives as the main source of their income. They widely use them in their daily life, making furniture for their houses with olive tree trunks and decorating it with palm fronds. The Siwan kitchen also widely uses palms and olives in many recipes as they even make olive jam (El-Bey 2016).

The Egyptian drama introduced some details about the marriage traditions in Siwa through T.V. series called "Sunset Oasis". It showed that according to the Siwan traditions, the bride prepares for her wedding by going with her friends to the hot spring water where she takes her bath alone in the spring while they sing and dance for her. Then, they took her to her family's house to wear the marriage traditional dress and they stay with her singing and dancing the whole night until the father of the bridegroom comes to take her to her bridegroom. Her brother carries her on his back all the way as her feet are not supposed to touch the ground until she arrives at her bed in her groom's house. The groom also prepares to the wedding similarly as he takes a hot spring bath while his friends celebrate with traditional singing and dancing and when he knows that his bride arrived at his house, he goes to meet her while his friends try to prevent him from entering his house as a Siwan tradition to prove the strength of the groom (Abu Zikry 2017).

The Siwan woman usually pays good attention to her personal adornment that she wears at home using colorful glass beads and embroiders. The traditional clothes consist of several layers of colorful dresses covered with the outer black dress embroidered with colorful silk threads. The wedding dress in Siwa is not just one dress as it consists of 7 layers of different dresses. Hence, the Siwan bride wears seven dresses at one time. Usually, the first layer is translucent white dress, the second is translucent red, the third is black, the fourth is yellow, the fifth is blue, the sixth is pink silk, and the outer seventh is embroidered around the neck, and a shawl of red silk is placed on the bride's head (Othman n.d.). The following picture in Fig. 6 shows those traditional dresses.

Among the Siwa's traditions related to marriage, for the first weeks of her marriage, the Siwan bride keeps wearing her golden

⟨Figure 6⟩ Traditional clothes of Siwan women

jewelry at home with special traditional dresses that she usually changes once or twice daily. She has to stay with her husband's family for the first two months of her marriage and limit her social visits so that she adapts to her new life learning from her mother in law house management. After this period of adaptation, according to the Siwan custom, the pride returns to her family and stays with them for one week, and her husband should prepare for this visit with gifts for her family including a sheep as a special gift for his father-in-law. During that week, the husband's family also visits the bride's family with gifts like foodstuff, sweets, and money. This supposes to strengthen the relationships between the two families newly united (Vale 2014, 194).

According to Siwan traditions, girls usually get engaged at the age of nine years to get married at the age of fifteen. Therefore, the girls are raised for the target of marriage so most of them escape education and usually graduate only middle school to start their early marriage. The decision of marriage and choosing the proper bridegroom is all up to the father of the girl. Since legally the age of marriage in Egypt is eighteen, in Siwa they make tribal marriage witnessed by the tribe, then later register the marriage when the girl is eighteen years old (Mokhtar 2012). This way early marriage, which is usually consanguineous marriage, continues according to the tribal rule in Siwa. This increases the health problems of children in Siwa Oasis.

3. Nubia

⟨Figure 7⟩ The Location of Nubia regions

Nubia is an ancient region extending into South Egypt and North Sudan. Its approximate location is starting in the Nile valley of Upper Egypt from the first cataract southward to the sixth cataract near Khartoum, the Sudanese capital. The Nubian region is traditionally divided into two regions of Upper Nubia in the southern part and Lower Nubia in the north. The Egyptian part is the Lower Nubia located between the first and the second cataracts of the Nile in the city of Aswan (Editors of Encyclopaedia 2022).

Many of the Nubians, who are indigenous ethnolinguistic groups of this region, live in the Egyptian city of Aswan as the Egyptian Nubia is located in the southern part of Aswan. The Nubian lands have been affected by the building of dams in Aswan resulting in the loss of about 60% of their lands in South Egypt. Over 45 Nubian villages were razed displacing their inhabitants and relocating them mainly to Kom Ombo, a village at the north of Aswan city. Some of them also moved to Cairo and other cities of Egypt (El-Akkad 2016).

The Nubians maintained their distinctive culture which can be noticed in their language, music, dance, songs, architecture, foods, clothes, and traditions. The colorful decorations in their houses with their special architecture attract many Egyptians and tourists to enjoy the Nubian arts. This made some hotels and restaurants in Egypt adopt the Nubian style introducing their unique culture. The following pictures of Fig. 8 show the Nubian architecture and arts in guest houses introducing the Nubian culture in Nubia of Aswan.

〈Figure 8〉 Nubian Houses Architecture

In the past, Nubian marriage ceremonies lasted for more than a week and sometimes lasted for 40 days. Nowadays, it takes only two or three days due to economic difficulties. Those ceremonies include celebrating the acceptance of the marriage among the two families as the groom presents gifts to the family of his bride while celebrating that day. There is also a celebration of furnishing the newlywed house, singing, and dancing while transferring the new furniture inside the house. The day before the wedding, which is the day for henna ceremonies, usually starts with slaughtering a cow or a sheep to be among other traditional food and cookies made for celebrations. As Nubia is famous for gold, the marriage gift "shabka" is golden jewelry and also the bride's family provides their daughter with golden jewels according to the Nubian traditions (Shehata 2017).

The henna day is one of the most important ceremonies before the wedding as Nubians are famous for their traditional henna arts. On the henna day which is the day before the wedding, the groom also has the traditional ceremony of painting his body with henna without drawing as it is only for moisturizing and softly coloring his body and they believe it protects him from evil eyes. Usually, an old lady of the groom's relative; like his grandmother or aunt, do this ceremony for him while his friends are attending celebrating, and singing for their friends. They also take some of the remaining henna after the groom finishes his henna anointing as a gesture of their wish to get married like their friend. Then all invitees give money to congratulate the groom while one of his friends writes down their names and the amounts each invitee gave so that those amounts will be paid back to them on future occasions (Abdel Rehiem 2009, 32). The following picture of Fig. 9 shows the bride and groom dressed in traditional Nubian clothes after henna ceremonies. Traditionally, the bride wears a red dress with golden jewelry and the groom wears a white galabia with a red shawl. The Nubian groom also preserves the tradition of wearing in his right hand a special bracelet made of red threads with a white shell, as seen in the following pictures of Fig. 9, believed to protect him from envy and evil eyes.

On the wedding day, the groom prepares by bathing in the Nile River similar to what grooms of Siwa oasis do in the spring water. Before reaching the river, the groom runs ahead of his friends, and each of them is keen not to precede the groom so that he should

⟨Figure 9⟩ Nubian traditions in henna ceremonies

be the winner on that day. After his bath in the river, the groom wears his new clothes for the wedding and gives his old clothes to one of the poor elderly people of the village, then the groom goes to his house among his friends to celebrate him singing and also saying prayers of Quran for blessing him. Then they accompany the groom to his bride's house. While they are on their way, they should pass by seven houses where they stop to celebrate by singing and dancing for the groom and giving also gifts to people they meet. At the bride's house, they continue the celebrations dancing and singing with the bride's family and other friends gathering there (Abdel Rehiem 2009).

These celebrations of the wedding last the whole night till the morning. The celebration usually ends in the morning as the groom has his breakfast with his friends at the house of the bride. Contrary to the traditions of Siwa oasis, the Nubian traditions recommend that the newlywed couple stays for the first week in the house of the bride's family. The Nubian marriage, also similar to Siwan marriage, is consanguineous marriage among relatives to preserve tribal ties, and in many cases, the couple is promised to get married from their childhood (Shehata 2017).

The traditional Nubian dance and singing accompanying all these marriage celebrations are well known for drumming on tambourines with group dances in lines. The following pictures of Fig. 10 show

⟨Figure 10⟩ Nubian Marriage Celebrations

those traditional tambourines used for Nubian songs and Nubians dressed in traditional clothes in one of those group dancing at Nubian weddings.

4. Sinai

The Sinai Peninsula, the eastern gate of Egypt, is the Asian part of the Egyptian territories. The map in Fig. 11 shows the location of the Sinai Peninsula in Egypt.

The Sinai Bedouins consist of many tribes, some of them are indigenous people of this land and some are Arabs who settled since the Arab conquest. Their language is Arabic like other Egyptians, but their dialect similar to the Levant dialect (Shokeir 2018).

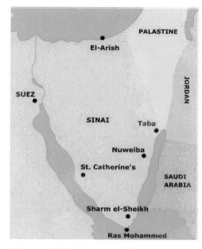

⟨Figure 11⟩ The Location of Sinai Peninsula

Each tribe has its marriage traditions that can differ from other tribes, but the general trend is that they persist in consanguineous marriage keeping their tribal ties strong. The Bedouin tradition gives priority to the cousin, who is the son of the father's brother, for marriage rather than other relatives. Early marriage is also traditionally adopted by Sinai Bedouins as they prefer marriage in an early age. They also facilitate the marriage by dividing the amount of Mahr, the money given to the bride, in installments to encourage the young men to get married earlier. So, the age for marriage is usually eighteen to twenty for men and sixteen to eighteen for girls (Imam 2013, 203, 220). Despite that the tradition impose arranged marriage by the families, the Bedouin society is full of many love stories. Usually, the Bedouin girl is brought up knowing the priority of her cousin to be her future husband. Thus, many girls naturally fell in love with their cousins before marriage. Other cases include falling in love with persons who are not welcomed by their families leading to tragic love stories ending without marriage (Imam 2013, 214-215).

As for the costs of marriage, which are relatively less than in other regions of Egypt due to the simplicity of the Bedouin life, the groom pays for all the costs of marriage according to the traditions of the Bedouins of Sinai. Thus, the groom provides the house, which was traditionally a tent in the past, with all the required furniture and he even pays for new marriage clothes of his bride. The wedding also is arranged by the groom. The bride is only preparing the henna celebration. All the celebrations are held in tents, so the wedding requires two big tents for celebrations, one for women and the other for men (Alshawadfy 2021).

As for Shabka, the jewelry gift, the Sinai Bedouins have their special designs of Jewels. In the past, traditionally the Shabka was silver bracelets of special designs, nine beads of 21k gold that the bride put in her burqa (traditional face cover), and a golden belt, which is the most expensive of this jewelry that can be delayed till the groom can buy it after marriage. However, nowadays girls prefer to receive more golden jewelry like rings or necklaces. The father of the bride also has to buy her some golden jewelry with some money from her mahr before marriage (Imam 2013, 244). The pictures in Fig. 12 show the unique designs of Sinai jewelry.

Sinai Burqa with beads of golds   Sinai designs for burqa jewel and necklace

〈Figure 12〉 Sinai jewelry for Shabka

The marriage celebrations extend for three days starting with henna day similar to other Egyptians, then the wedding day, and the celebration extends to the first day after the wedding. On the wedding day, families and friends gather at night to enjoy the moonlight while singing traditional songs and dancing. Also, poem reciting is one of the traditions included in those night celebrations (Zayed 2021).

The Sinai wedding dress is as special as the bride starts to make it and embroider it by herself with red threads since puberty. So, the making of the Sinai wedding dress takes a long time with care and patience to be ready quite long before the wedding day (Imam 2013, 260). The following picture of Fig. 13 shows the Sinai wedding dress.

Sinai traditional wedding dress
Sinai Women in traditional clothes

〈Figure 13〉 Sinai traditional clothes with red embroidery

The Bedouin marriage celebrations differ from past to present. In the past, the girls did not know to whom they got married or when, as the tradition was that the groom's family come on camels to take the bride surprisingly to her groom while she is doing her normal work herding the sheep, so she usually resists this act due to the sudden change happening to her life and fearing that new life. According to this tradition, neither the father of the bride nor the groom participates while taking her to her new home. However, this tradition changed at present, as the bride now knows previously her groom and the time of her wedding day, but still, her father and her groom should not accompany her while she is transferring to her new house, as the groom should wait for her coming in their house, and her father should not witness this moment that she is taken to another house as a symbol of changing her protector from her father to the groom. Also, the tradition persists from the past that the bride shows resistance to going with her groom's family while she screams asking for the help of her family. It is not proper for the bride to go without resistance. According to their traditions, if she does not show resistance, she will be criticized for showing eagerness for marriage. So, in some cases, her resistance leads them to tie her with robes to enforce her to go with them (Imam 2013, 264-267).

During the celebrations which extend to the first day after marriage, the feasts are prepared with traditional food and slaughtering sheep for the invitees who also help in those feasts by presenting gifts of food, sheep, and goats for the newlywed couple. Those celebrations usually end with the feasts of lunch meal shared on the first day of the marriage (Imam 2013, 280-282). The joyful celebrations of marriage can be seen commonly among those groups in Egypt including traditional singing and dancing, wearing traditional clothes, and showing generosity by providing traditional foods for guests slaughtering an animal, usually sheep. The henna ceremony also is something appeared to be common for marriage celebrations of most Egyptians regardless of social or economic differences.

IV. Conclusion

Egypt has a unique mix of history and modernity with a variety of rich cultures. Tracing the marriage concept in Egypt, we saw the strong influence of religion giving holiness to this commitment. Social custom also plays an important role in forming this concept regarding marriage. Even, sometimes social custom has a stronger influence than religion, which can be seen in the continuity of pre-Islamic customs and traditions to the present.

In this context, early marriage and consanguineous marriage can be seen more adopted in rural areas and among Bedouin and ethnic groups in Egypt. The social customs can be seen as a factor behind as seen in the cases of Nubians, Sinai Bedouins, and Siwan Amazighs. The educational level also contributes to the formation of those concepts. Thus, in big cities, like Cairo, where education is more developed, these phenomena of early marriage and consanguineous marriage are decreasing. Westernization also has an influence on Cairenes adopting more western life as seeing their weddings and marriage arrangements.

Egyptian society is rich in cultural diversity seeing the different cultural groups still preserving their traditions for hundreds of years. Among those groups, we introduced the Amazigh of Siwa, Nubians of Aswan, and Bedouins of Sinai. Each of those groups had maintained its distinctive traditions from the past till today seen in their marriage arrangements and celebrations. Each group has their traditional arts seen in their unique designs of architecture, music, songs, dance, clothes, music, or jewels. Their marriage customs also survived through time as seen in many customs still preserved proudly showing their appreciation for their history and culture.

References

Abdel Rehiem, Ahmed. 2009. "Marriage celebration for Nubians (احتفالية الزواج عند النوبيين)." *Folk Culture* 5. pp. 30-39.

Abdou, Mona. May 15, 2022. "The Unseen World of Egypt's Siwi Berber." https://egyptianstreets. com/2022/05/15/the-unseen-world-of-egypts-siwi-berber/ (accessed Aug. 27, 2022).

Sunset Oasis. 2017. Directed by Kamla Abu Zikry. Produced by Taher, Bahaa.

Allam, Sara. Nov. 18, 2019. "Deputy Patriarch of Catholics: Our laws prevent the marriage of cousins, uncles and aunts, and allow them on condition (نائب بطريرك الكاثوليك:قوانيننا تمنع زواج أبناء العمة والعم والخلة والسماح بها بشرط)." https://www.youm7.com/story/2019/11/18/%D9%86%D8%A7%D8%A6%D8%A8-%D8%A8%D8%B7%D8%B1%D9%8A%D8%B1%D9%83-%D8%A7%D9%84%D9%83%D8%A7%D8%AB%D9%88%D9%84%D9%8A%D9%83-%D9%82%D9%88%D8%A7%D9%86%D9%8A%D9%86%D9%86%D8%A7-%D8%AA%D9%85%D9%86%D8%B9-%D8%B2%D9%88%D8%A7%D8%AC-(accessed Aug. 21, 2022).

Alshawadfy, Hamadah. June 7, 2021. "Marriage of South Sinai Bedouins (الزواج عند بدو جنوب سيناء)." https://www.elwatannews.com/news/details/5521317 (accessed Sep. 4, 2022).

Bernard-Maugiron, Nathalie. 2010. *Promotion of Women's Rights (Egypt): Personal Status Laws in Egypt*. Cairo: German Technical Cooperation (GTZ).

Editors of Encyclopaedia. April 15, 2022. "Nubia." *Britannica*. https://www.britannica. com/place/Nubia (accessed Aug. 31, 2022).

El-Akkad, Farah. Oct. 25, 2016. "52 Years After Displacement, Scars Of Loss Remain For Nubians." *Egypt Today*. https://www.egypttoday.com/Article/10/3182/52-Years-After-Displacement-Scars-Of-Loss-Remain-For-Nubians (accessed Aug. 31, 2022).

El-Bey, Doaa. Oct. 27, 2016. "Exploring Egypt: The fascinating face of Siwa Oasis." *Ahram online*. https://english.ahram.org.eg/NewsPrint/246616.aspx (accessed Aug. 31, 2022).

El-Shamma, Mohamed. July 14, 2019. "High marriage costs cause slump in Egyptian weddings." https://www.arabnews.com/node/1525181/middle-east (accessed Aug. 22, 2022).

El-Tawila, S., and Z. Khadr. 2004. *Patterns of Marriage and Family Formation among Youth in Egypt.* Cairo: National Population Council, Center for Information and Computer Systems, Faculty of Economics and Political Science, Cairo University.

Encyclopaedia Britannica. 2015. "Nubia: Ancient region of Nubia." *Encyclopaedia Britannica.* https://www.britannica.com/biography/Sesostris-II (accessed Aug. 31, 2022).

Hammad, Manal B. 2009. "Siwa Oasis: A Neglected Paradise." *3rd IRT International Scientific Conference: Integrated Relational Tourism Territories and Development in the Mediterranean Area.* Cairo: Helwan University. pp. 765-772.

Imam, Nahlah. 2013. *Good day: Marriage customs of the Sinai Bedouins* (عادات: زين النهار الزواج لدى بدو سيناء). Cairo: General Authority for Cultural Palaces.

Mamdouh, Amira. Sep. 8, 2021. "Cairo and Alexandria are the highest in the age of marriage, and Upper Egypt is at the bottom of the list (القاهرة والإسكندرية الأعلى فى سن الزواج والصعيد يتذيل القائمة)." https://www.dostor.org/3564113#:~:text=%D9%83%D8%B4%D9%81%20 %D8%A7%D9%84%D8%AC%D9%87%D8%A7%D8%B2%20%D8%A7%D9%84% D9%85%D8%B1%D9%83%D8%B2%D9%89%20%D9%84%D9%84%D8%AA%D- 8%B9%D8%A8%D8%A6%D8%A9%20%D8%A7%D9%84%D8%B9%D8%A7%D9% 85%D8%A9,%D8%B3%D9%86%D8%A9%20%D9%8828 (accessed Aug. 21, 2022).

Mokhtar, Yomna. Nov. 11, 2012. "Here is Siwa (هنا سيوة)." https://www.almasryalyoum. com/news/details/240332 (accessed Aug. 30, 2022).

Othman, Soheir. "Egyptian Traditions and Customs: Siwa Oasis." n.d. http://www.kenanaonline.net/page/4790 (accessed Aug. 31, 2022).

Shehata, Amira. June 27, 2017. "The most beautiful ceremonies of Nubian weddings from Aswan to Cairo (أجمل طقوس أفراح النوبيين من أسوان للقاهرة)." https://www.youm7.com/story/2017/ 6/27/%D8%A3%D8%AC%D9%85%D9%84-%D8%B7%D9%82%D9%88%D8%B3- %D8%A3%D9%81%D8%B1%D8%A7%D8%AD-%D8%A7%D9%84%D9 %86%D9%88%D8%A8%D9%8A%D9%8A%D9%86-%D9%85%D9%86- %D8%A3%D8%B3%D9%88%D8%A7%D9%86-%D9%84%D9%84%D9%82%D8% A7%D9%87%D8%B1%D8%A9-(accessed Sep. 3, 2022).

Shokeir, Naom. 2018. *History of Sinai and Arab* (تاريخ سيناء والعرب). Cairo: Hindawi org.

Singerman, Diane. 2008. "Marriage and Divorce in Egypt: Financial Costs and Political Struggles." In *Les Métamorphoses du Mariage au Moyen-Orient*, edited by Barbara Drieskens, 75-96. Beirut: Presses de l'Ifpo.

The Editors of Encyclopaedia. Feb. 24, 2016. "Siwa Oasis." *Encyclopedia Britannica.* https://www.britannica.com/place/Siwa-Oasis (accessed Aug. 27, 2022).

UNICEF. 2017. *Egypt Country Brief: Child Marriage in the Middle East and North Africa.* Amman: United Nations Children's Fund (UNICEF), Regional Office for the Middle East and North Africa.

Vale, Margaret M. 2014. *Siwa: Jewelry, Costume, and Life in an Egyptian Oasis.* Oxford: Oxford University Press.

Yusri, Mohamed. Aug. 23, 2008. "The Sinai Embroidered Dress (الثوب السيناوي المطرز)." *The Middle East.* https://archive.aawsat.com/details.asp?section=54&article=483973&issueno=10861#.YxWY9HZBxPY (accessed Sep. 5, 2022).

Zayed, Said. June 26, 2021. "Marriage in North Sinai..between simplicity and originality (الزواج في شمال سيناء.. بين البساطة والاصالة)." *Dar Elhilal.* https://darelhilal.com/News/841287.aspx (accessed Sep. 4, 2022).

Image Source

〈Figure 1〉 Encyclopaedia Britannica. 2012

〈Figure 2〉 SomethingBorrowed. "19 Facts About Wedding Rings History." n.d. https://somethingborrowedpdx.com/history-of-wedding-rings/ (accessed Aug. 22, 2022).

〈Figure 3〉 Almasry Alyoum. June 16, 2018. "Weddings of Copts." https://www.almasryalyoum.com/news/details/1300429 (accessed Aug. 23, 2022).

〈Figure 4〉 Alfio. January 23 , 2010. "CIA World Factbook maps of Egypt." Wikimedia Commons. https://commons.wikimedia.org/wiki/Category:CIA_World_Factbook_maps_of_Egypt#/media/File:Eg-map-sv.png (accessed Aug. 27, 2022).

〈Figure 5〉 Hermann, Michael. March 10, 2016. "Siwa Oasis, Egypt." https://commons.wikimedia.org/wiki/File:Shali_(Historic_Center_of_Siwa)_02.JPG (accessed Aug. 29, 2022).

〈Figure 6〉 Abdel-Qader, El-Sayed. Dec. 3, 2018. "Siwi dress is challenging the world's fashion." https://gate.ahram.org.eg/daily/Media/News/2018/12/2/2018-636793840330284182-28.jpg (accessed Aug. 29, 2022).

〈Figure 7〉 Encyclopaedia Britannica 2015

〈Figure 8〉 Mashaly, Abdullah. May 14, 2021. "Nubian meals price in Aswan." Elwatan News. https://www.elwatannews.com/news/details/5489319 (accessed Sep. 1, 2022).

〈Figure 9〉 Yousef. July 25, 2011. "Modern Nubian Wedding (الفـــرح النـــوبي الحـــديث)." http://alnubakorsel.blogspot.com/2011/07/blog-post_24.html (accessed Sep. 1, 2022).

Waheesh, Mostafa. June 9, 2017. "Nubian beliefs: red threads and a white shell to protect the groom (معتقدات نوبية خيوط حمراء وقوقعة بيضاء لحماية العريس)." https://akhbarelyom.com/news/newdetails/2508707/1/%D9%85%D8%B9%D8%AA%D9%82%D8%AF%D8%A7%D8%AA-%D9%86%D9%88%D8%A8%D9%8A%D8%A9-%D8%AE%D9%8A%D9%88%D8%B7-%D8%AD%D9%85%D8%B1%D8%A7%D8%A1-%D9%88%D9%82%D9%88%D9%82%D8%B9%D8%A9-%D8%A8%D9%8A%D8%B6%D8%A7%D8%A1-%D9%84% (accessed Sep. 3, 2022).

⟨Figure 10⟩ Samir, Nahed. June 7, 2012. "Rani revives the heritage of the Nuba with the tambourine and the tambour (راني يحيى تراث النوبة بالدف والطنبور)." Alwatan. https://www.elwatannews.com/news/details/24442 (accessed Sep. 3, 2022).

Salah, Abdallah. Dec. 19, 2017. "Pictures..Nuba rises up against the high cost of dowries (صور..النوبة تنتفض ضد غلاء المهور)." https://www.youm7.com/story/2017/12/19/%D8%B5%D9%88%D8%B1-%D8%A7%D9%84%D9%86%D9%88%D8%A8%D8%A9-%D8%AA%D9%86%D8%AA%D9%81%D8%B6-%D8%B6%D8%AF-%D8%BA%D9%84%D8%A7%D8%A1-%D8%A7%D9%84%D9%85%D9%87%D9%88%D8%B1-%D8%A7%D9%84%D8%B4%D8%A8%D8%A7%D8%A8-%D9%8A%D8%B7%D9%8 (accessed Aug. 31, 2022).

⟨Figure 11⟩ Eid, Tolba. "Tolba Desert Tour." n.d. http://www.tolbatours.com/enSinai.html (accessed Sep. 5, 2022).

⟨Figure 12⟩ Ayman, Karma. May 25, 2017. "Sinai Embroidery Guide (دليل التطريز السيناوي)." https://m.masralarabia.net/ (accessed Sep. 5, 2022).

Hefny, Rania. Oct. 30, 2015. "Egyptian clothes and jewelry (الملابس والحلي المصرية)." https://gate.ahram.org.eg/daily/News/131708/112/449677/%D8%A8%D8%B1-%D9%85%D8%B5%D8%B1/%D9%85%D9%86%D9%87%D8%A7-%D8%A7%D9%84%D8%AE%D9%84%D8%AE%D8%A7%D9%84-%D9%88%D8%A7%D9%84%D9%83%D8%B1%D8%AF%D8%A7%D9%86-%D9%88%D9%82%D9%84%D8%A7%D8%A6%D8%AF-%D8%A7%D9%84%D (accessed Sep. 5, 2022).

⟨Figure 13⟩ Alaa Eldin, Dina. Dec. 8, 2010. "Bazar Sinawi." https://kenanaonline.com/files/0019/19090/large_1238028122[1].jpg (accessed Sep. 5, 2022).

Yusri, Mohamed. Aug. 23, 2008. "The Sinai Embroidered Dress (الثوب السيناوي المطرز)." *The Middle East*. https://archive.aawsat.com/details.asp?section=54&article=483973&issueno=10861#.YxWY9HZBxPY (accessed Sep. 5, 2022)

3부

요르단의 결혼 문화
(Marriage Culture in Jordan)

진소영

(부산외대 아랍학과)

지중해 동부에 위치한 요르단의 정식 국명은 요르단 하심 왕국 (Hashemite Kingdom of Jordan)이다. 국민의 약 95%가 무슬림이며, 약 4%의 기독교인과 기타 소수 종교로 구성되어 있다. 요르단은 다른 이슬람 국가에 비해 타 종교에 개방적인 편이다. 종교 차별 금지법을 헌법으로 제정하고 종교를 기반으로 한 정당을 금지함으로써, 정치인들은 세속주의를 추구한다. 물론 이교도에 관용적일지라도 요르단의 사회문화는 이슬람교의 영향을 크게 받을 수밖에 없으며, 지면에서 다루고자 할 결혼문화도 예외는 아니다.

중동 이슬람 문화에서 일반적으로 나타나는 공통점은 결혼 적령기의 남녀가 배우자를 직접 선택하지 않고 주로 부모에 의해 결정된다는 점이다. 아버지의 종교가 자녀에게 상속되기 때문에 무슬림 남성은 비무슬림 여성과의 결혼이 허용되는 반면, 무슬림 여성은 반드시 무슬림 남성과 결혼해야 한다. 만약 무슬림 여성이 비무슬림 남성과 결혼하려면 남자는 결혼 전 무슬림으로 개종해야 한다. 이 부분은 남녀 차별로 느껴질 수 있겠으나, 이를 제외하고 실제 이슬람 문화권에서 결혼은 여성의 동격성과 자립성을 확보하는데 중요한 의미가 있다.

이슬람법에 의해 여성은 자신의 사유재산에 대해 절대적인 권리를 행사한다. 대표적으로 결혼 시 신랑이 신부에게 일정 금액의 재화를 지불하는 '마흐르(mahr)'라는 혼납금이 있다. 마흐르는 요르단을 비롯한 이슬람 문화권에서 흔히 볼 수 있는 결혼 전통일 뿐만 아니라 여성 무슬림의 법적 권리이기도 하다. 마흐르는 남편과의 이혼, 사망 등 불가피한 상황에서 여성 자신을 위한 최소한의 복지금으로 사용할 수 있다. 보통 신랑의 경제적 능력과 신부의 상황에 따라 액수가 정해지며, 현금, 귀금속, 부동산 등 어느 형태로 지급되어도 무방하다. 마흐르는 결혼 후 전적으로 신부 소유가 되며, 남편은 부인의 어떤 사유재산에도 간여할 수 없다. 뿐만 아니라 이슬람 문화권에서는 결혼 후 부인이 남편의 성을 따르지 않고 본인의 성을 간직할 수 있다.

요르단에서 결혼은 신랑과 신부, 두 사람의 결합뿐만 아니라 가족 집단주의를 의미한다. 특히 요르단과 같은 집단주의 사회에서는 결혼 문제에 부모 또는 집안의 영향력이 클 수밖에 없으며 개인의 일이 아닌 집안의 일로 간주한다.

과거의 결혼 조건은 철저히 집안 배경을 바탕으로 한 양가의 합의에 따른 행사였다. 대부분 혼례는 카티바(khatiba, 신랑 집안의 요구로 적합한 신부를 찾아주는 중매 여성)의 주선으로 성사됐다. 카티바의 소개로 남성은 여성의 집을 방문하고 신부가 마음에 들면 청혼한다. 신랑과 신부가 만나는 장소에는 항상 여자 가족 측의 보호자인 '마흐람(mahram)'이 동석해야 한다. 마흐람은 아버지, 남자 형제, 삼촌, 조카와 같이 이슬람 율법에서 혼인을 허용하지 않는 가까운 친척을 의미한다. 마흐람이 동행하는 이유는 남녀 간에 일어날 수 있는 부도덕한 일을 방지하기 위해서다. 결혼이 이루어지면 양측 모두가 카티바에게 수수료를 지급한다. 당시 카티바는 보수적인 아랍 사회에서 배우자를 찾을 수 있는 유일한 원천이었다. 전통적으로 카티바는 그 마을에서 가장 덕망이 높은 사람이 할 수 있으며, 양가의 사회적 신분, 재산, 직업,

결혼 당사자의 교육 수준 등을 고려해 혼담을 진행한다.

오늘날은 과거에 비해 남녀의 만남이 자유로워져 카티바의 역할이 점차 줄어들고 있다. 21세기의 결혼은 집안이나 지인 소개로 이뤄지는 중매 결혼과 연애 결혼으로 나뉘지만, 당사자가 좋아한다고 해서 곧바로 결혼으로 이어지지는 않는다. 반드시 양가 부모의 허락을 얻어야 하는 것이 일반적이다.

최근에는 배우자의 학벌이나 나이, 집안의 명성 및 재력, 외모, 성격 등이 결혼의 주요 요건이지만, 일반적으로 남자가 여자보다 나이가 많거나 학벌이 높은 쪽을 선호하는 편이다. 결혼식은 양가 남성의 협의로 이루어지는데 주로 마흐르 액수 책정, 약혼식과 결혼식 장소 확정 및 비용 부담 등 결혼 제반에 따른 대화가 오간다. 요르단을 포함한 이슬람 문화권에서 결혼의 규모는 그 가문의 명예와 평판을 판가름하기에 대부분 호화로운 결혼식을 선호한다.

I. 요르단에서 결혼의 의미와 기능

결혼이란 남녀가 만나 부부가 되고 새로운 가정을 이루어 나가는 인생의 출발점이다. 일생일대의 중대사인 결혼은 각 나라의 문화와 전통에 따라 다양한 특징을 갖고 있다. 요르단의 결혼은 지역마다 조금씩 다른 형태를 띠지만, 현대 사회에 이르러서는 베두인족의 전통 결혼식은 거의 사라졌다. 대신 서구 문화의 유입에 따라 서구식 결혼식이 증가하고 있다. 과거에는 결혼식이 양가 집안의 결합을 축하하는 의미였다면, 오늘날 결혼식은 서구적인 화려함과 형식을 중히 여기는 이벤트로 변화하고 있다.

2014년 경제연구포럼(Economic Research Forum) 통계에 따르면 요

르단의 평균 결혼 비용은 14,000달러인데 반해, 요르단인의 평균 급여는 월 500달러로 나타났다. 요르단 여성의 평균 결혼 연령은 24세, 남성은 29세이다. 마흐르와 결혼식 비용 그리고 주거지 마련 비용에 이르기까지 결혼에 대한 재정적 의무는 전통적으로 남자에게 있다. 2016년 요르단 여성위원회 (The Jordanian National Commission for Women) 통계에 의하면 혼납금은 2,174디나르 (약 3,066달러)이다.

신랑과 신부는 가족이나 친구로부터 냉장고, 세탁기, 청소기, TV 등 신혼 집에 필요한 가전 등을 선물로 받으며, 신부가 신랑보다 더 많은 선물을 받는 편이다. 가까운 친척들은 신부에게 보석류나, 금반지, 금목걸이, 금팔찌와 같은 금붙이를 선물한다. 금을 주는 이유는 현금과 같은 효과가 있어 신부의 재정적인 안정에 도움이 될 수 있기 때문이다.

Ⅱ. 요르단의 결혼 방식

이슬람은 무슬림 남성이 최다 4명까지 부인을 둘 수 있는 일부다처제를 허용한다. 일부다처제가 생겨난 배경은 부족 및 국가 간 전쟁이 빈번하고 사회복지 제도가 없던 당시, 남편이 전사할 경우 살아남은 형제가 결혼을 통해 생계가 어려워진 유족을 돌보게 하려는 배려에서였다. 같은 이슬람권이지만 다처제를 허용하는 국가가 있고 금지하는 국가가 있다. 요르단에서는 무슬림이 4명의 아내를 맞이하는 것이 합법이다. 하지만 2017~2018년, 15세~49세 기혼 남성을 대상으로 실시한 '인구 및 가족 건강 조사'에 따르면 남성의 1%만이 한 명 이상의 여성과 결혼했다는 통계가 나왔다.

모든 국가가 결혼에 관한 고유의 관습과 전통을 가지고 있다는 것은 의심의 여지가 없다. 요르단의 결혼 제도도 마찬가지이다. 오늘날 요르단 결혼식을 보면 이슬람 문화권의 결혼식과 크게 다르지는 않지만, 그들만의 결혼 문화가 스며들어 있음을 알 수 있다. 요르단의 전통 결혼은 여러 단계를 거치는데, 보편적으로 결혼식 전후로 자하, 약혼식, 헤나의 밤, 청년의 밤, 왈리마 행사가 거행된다.

① 결혼 절차

– 자하 (jaha)

요르단의 첫 번째 혼례 절차는 '자하'다. 신랑과 그의 친척으로 구성된 사람들이 신붓집에 와서 청혼을 하는 행위를 말한다. 신부 측 가족이 신랑 측 가족의 청혼을 받아들일 것인지 가늠해 보는 과정이라고도 할 수 있다. 아울러 혼례 준비 과정에서 가족이나 다른 구성원 사이에서 발생할 수 있는 분쟁을 원만하게 해결하고자 미리 상의하는 의미도 있다. 약혼 전, 서로에 대한 존중의 정도를 나타내는 것이다.

'자하'는 두 사람을 결혼시키기 위해 모인 남성 그룹으로 남녀의 부모, 조부모, 증조부 또는 집안의 친척 어른, 가까운 친구 등으로 구성되는데 이는 가족 간의 합의를 상징한다.

집안의 어른들로 구성된 신랑 대표단은 신부의 집으로 향한다. 여자 측 가족의 연장자가 남자 측을 기다리고 있다. 파견단은 10명 이하일 수도 있고, 어떤 경우에는 수백 명일 수도 있다. 이때 신랑 측에서 신부 측으로 가는 '자하'의 인원이 많을수록 신랑 가족의 명예와 지위가 높아진다. 신부 가족의 남자들이 줄을 서서 신랑 측 손님을 맞이한다. 신랑 신부의 각 대표와 악수를 하고 인사를 교환한다. 마주 보는 의자에 자리를 잡고 나머지 손님들이 입장할 때까지 기다린다. 모두가 좌석에 앉으면 여자 측에서 남자 측 대표 연사에게 아랍 커피를 제공한다.

자하를 위해 대표 연사는 신부 측 가족에게 남성과 남성측 가문을 소개한 후 결혼과 관련된 꾸란의 구절과 하디스의 구절을 암송하며 결혼을 요청한다. 이때 연사는 신부 측 가족의 최종 결혼 동의를 얻을 때까지 커피를 마시지 않는다. 신부와 가족이 수락할 때까지 기다렸다가 긍정적인 반응을 얻으면 커피를 마시는 것이 관례다. 수락의 의도로 꾸란 개경장을 읽고, 신랑의 가족 및 모든 구성원과 악수하며 마무리 한다.

이후 과자, 쿠나파(Knafeh)와 같은 아랍식 디저트와 초콜릿 등이 차려진다. 오늘날에는 '자하'를 신부의 집이 아닌 호텔이나 큰 홀을 빌려서 하는 경우도 있다.

자하가 성공적으로 끝나면 약혼 축하 행사가 열린다. 남성과 여성은 공식적으로 약혼을 하고, 하나가 된 두 가족은 작은 축하 파티를 연다. 남녀가 서로에 대해 알아가고, 그들의 감정을 확인하는 시간을 가진 후, 가족들은 결혼식 비용, 혼납금,[1] 신부의 예물 등에 관한 논의를 시작한다. 신부의 보석 선물은 요르단 결혼의 중요한 전통이다. 기본적으로 보석은 신부를 위한 금 액세서리를 의미한다. 일부 가정에서는 보석이 아닌 간소한 결혼반지를 요청하기도 한다.

---

1 마흐르는 남녀 가문의 사회적 평판에 상당한 영향을 미친다. 여성 측은 마흐르를 많이 받을수록 여성 측 가문에 대한 평가가 높아지고, 신랑 측은 마흐르를 많이 책정할수록 신랑 측 가문의 경제력뿐만 아니라 관대함을 간접적으로 나타나기 때문에 사회적 위신 또한 높아지기 때문이다. 따라서 마흐르는 양가의 체면과 명예에 의해 무리하게 책정되는 경우가 있다.

〈그림1〉 자하 사진1

〈그림2〉 자하 사진2

– 헤나의 밤(Laylat Al-Henna)과 청춘의 밤(Sahra Al-Shabab)

요르단에서는 신랑과 신부가 결혼식 전날 밤, 각각 잔치를 벌이는 것이 관례적이다. 신혼부부는 이날 각자 친구와 친척을 초대한다.

헤나 파티는 결혼식 하루 전에 열리는 여자들의 모임으로 보통 신부의 아버지 집에서 열린다. 신부는 전통적인 수를 놓은 드레스나 현대적 드레스를 입는다. 헤나의 밤은 '송별회'라고도 불리는데, 예전에는 결혼을 위해 가문을 떠난 여성을 쉽게 만날 수 없었기 때문에 생겨난 관습이다. 이날 신랑 집안의 여자들과 신부의 친구들은 결혼을 축하하기 위해 신부의 집으로 간다. 헤나의 밤에 초대된 사람들은 헤나를 반죽해서 꽃과 밀랍으로 장식된 접시에 담는다. 신부의 친구들과 가족은 신부의 손이나 발에 헤나를 그린다. 때로는 신부가 헤나 디자이너를 초대해서 특별한 헤나의 밤을 즐기기도 한다.

'청춘의 밤' 파티는 신랑의 아버지 집에서 열리며 신랑을 축하하기 위한 남자들의 모임이다. 남자들은 다브케(Dabkeh)와 같은 토착 민속춤으로 결혼 축하 파티를 한다. 이날은 신랑의 친구와 가까운 친척들이 결혼 첫날밤을 위해 신랑을 가꿔주는 날이기에 '샤워의 밤'이라고도 지칭한다.

〈그림3〉 헤나의 밤   〈그림4〉 요르단 민속춤인 다브케

- 결혼식

요르단에서 혼인신고를 하려면 샤리아(이슬람 율법) 법원을 통해야 한다. 신랑 신부는 법원에 각 가족 구성원을 소개하는 공식 문서인 가족 수첩, 신분증, 남자의 아내가 3명 이하임을 나타내는 증명서, 여성이 다른 남자의 양육권에 속해 있지 않음을 증명하는 제출서, 혼인 전 건강 검진서를 제출해야 한다. 최근에는 법원을 직접 방문하지 않고 인터넷으로 신청하고 서류를 제출하는 것으로 바뀌어 가는 추세다.

이슬람 문화권에서는 남성의 금과 비단 제품 사용을 금지하고 있다. 따라서 결혼반지는 여성은 금반지를, 남성은 은반지를 하는 것이 보편적이다.

과거 요르단의 결혼은 '자하'처럼 신랑 가족이 줄지어 신붓집으로 향했지만, 현대에 접어들면서 이 문화 역시 바뀌고 있다. 특히 호화로운 결혼식 장소를 찾는 경향이 있는데, 규모에 따라 신랑, 신부와 그 부모의 사회적 권위와 배경을 가늠할 수 있기 때문이다.

결혼식 날짜는 금요일을 가장 선호한다. 요르단에서 금요일은 종교, 사회적 의미에서 축복의 날로 여겨진다.

<그림5> 요르단의 혼인신고서 　　　　　　 <그림6> 온라인 혼인신고 홈페이지

　　결혼식 전에 신랑은 꽃들로 차를 장식한다. 공식 결혼식 날 신랑의 가족들
이 신부를 데리러 신붓집까지 차량 행렬을 이어가기 위함이다. 신랑의 아버
지나 삼촌은 베두인 전통 코트인 푸르와(furwa)를 입고 있는데, 이는 새 가
족이 될 신부를 위한 보호의 상징으로서 덮어주는 역할을 한다. 다음으로 신
부는 경적을 울리는 차량에 탑승, 자신의 가족과 함께 결혼식 장소로 이동한
다. 결혼식 장소로 가는 동안에 시끄러운 경적을 계속 울리지만, 요르단 사람
들은 이 문화를 이해한다. 결혼식장에 도착했을 때도 환영 연주가 이어진다.
기본적으로 '타블라'로 불리는 북을 주 악기로 하는 전통 밴드를 선호한다.
또한, 요르단 전통춤인 답카(dabke)춤으로 결혼의 흥을 돋운다. 다른 문화
권의 결혼식과 달리 요르단 결혼식에서는 선물을 교환하지 않고, 돈을 선물
한다. 요르단 전통문화에 따르면 신랑과 그의 가족은 모든 결혼 비용을 내며

신혼집을 장만해야 한다. 대신 약혼식 비용은 신부 측에서 정산하기도 한다.

결혼 예복은 전통의상에서부터 최신식 유행 스타일까지 다양하지만, 신랑 대부분은 턱시도를, 신부는 웨딩드레스를 입는다. 결혼을 축하하기 위해 총을 쏘는 풍습이 있는데, 오늘날에는 결혼식 영상 촬영, 불꽃놀이 등으로 대체되고 있다.

– 왈리마(Walima)

'왈리마'는 결혼 후 여는 피로연의 개념이다. 가정의 행복을 나타내는 상징으로, 요르단의 결혼 문화 중 가장 중요한 전통이다. 피로연의 주체는 신랑, 신부가 아닌 그들을 보살피는 가족 내 집단, 즉 부모나 형제, 친척이 되는 것이 보통이다. 과거에는 30일 동안 결혼을 축하하며 매일 음식이 제공됐지만, 최근에는 하루 혹은 며칠로 바뀌었다. 또한, 과거 피로연의 형태는 손수 음식을 만들어 고마운 마음을 전달했으나, 오늘날에는 출장뷔페나 식당 등에서 대접하는 문화로 바뀌고 있다. 대표적인 음식으로는 요르단의 주식인 '만사프'가 있다. 만사프는 양고기, 우유, 쌀, 슈라크(shrak)로 구성된 요리이다.

– 요르단 결혼 후 조식(Sabahia)

결혼식 다음 날 아침, 신랑의 어머니가 아들 부부를 방문한다. 신랑의 어머니는 신혼부부를 위해 푸짐한 아침을 요리하고, 저녁이 되면 신부의 어머니가 준비한 디저트를 먹으며 가족들이 행복한 시간을 보낸다. 하지만 오늘날에는 호텔 식사로 대체되고 있다.

– 결혼 전 건강 검진

요르단을 포함한 중동 이슬람 문화권에서는 사촌 간 혼인이 성행해왔다. 가족 간의 결합이 결혼생활의 조화를 보장해줄 수 있다고 여겼으며, 일반적으로 사촌 간 혼인일 경우 마흐르의 액수가 낮은 편이기 때문이다. 하지만 건강적인 측면에서 사촌 간의 혼인은 유전적 질병의 발현 위험이 크므로, 오늘날 중동 이슬람 문화권에서는 사촌 간 혼인에 앞서서 혼전 건강 검진을 권고한다. 요르단에서는 63.7%의 결혼이 혈연관계에 의해 이루어진다. 요르단 보건복지부에 따르면, 2004년부터 결혼을 원하는 모든 부부는 '혼전 건강 검진 제도'에 의해 혼인서약서에 서명하기 전, 의료센터에서 두 사람 사이의 유전적 일치 정도와 유전 질환이 없는지를 확인해야 한다. 진단 결과 남녀 모두가 '지중해 빈혈증(Thalassemia)' 또는 겸상적혈구빈혈 유전형질을 가지고 있는 것으로 판명될 경우, 유전자 상담이 이루어지며 출산의 위험성을 설명한다. 다만 이로 인해 혼인을 할 수 없는 것은 아니다. 그럼에도 당사자가 결혼을 원한다면 할 수 있다.

– 결혼식 비용(2021년 요르단의 결혼 비용)[2]

약혼 기간 동안 신랑은 신혼집을 마련하고, 신부는 새로운 출발에 필요한 모든 것을 구입하고 드레스를 준비한다. 오늘날 결혼식은 보통 예식장이나 호텔에서 치러지며, 초대장을 통해서 결혼식을 안내한다.

---

2   https://m3rfah.com/ (검색일 2022.09.03.)

요르단 평균 결혼식 비용	35,366$		결혼 반지	884$
신랑 양복 및 액세서리	120$		결혼 팔찌	197$
신부 결혼 드레스	1,409$	각종 보석류	귀걸이	171$
신부의 액세서리 (머리장식, 구두, 속옷 등)	259$		목걸이	225$
신부 웨딩헤어	61–101$	웨딩사진		1,891$
신부 화장	66$	청첩장 및 결혼 안내 비용		397$
스파 및 매니큐어	55$	양가 부모를 위한 선물		145$
꽃다발과 결혼식 장식	397$	결혼식 사회 및 댄스팀		767$

② 혼례복과 음식

- 혼례복

오늘날 신부는 전형적인 흰색 웨딩드레스를 입고 신랑은 검은색 정장을 입는다. 보다 전통적인 의상을 입을 경우 신부는 머리를 덮는 실크 천과 은 또는 금 장신구와 함께 수놓은 전통 드레스를 입는다. 보통 히잡이 달린 긴소매 웨딩드레스가 선호된다. 반면 신랑은 양복을 입는다. 만약 결혼식 하객으로 참석할 경우 노출이 많이 없고 단정한 긴바지와 치마를 착용하는 것이 좋다.

- 음식

결혼식 전날 저녁 식사는 지역에 따라 다르다. 북부 도시에서는 간 고기와 밀을 반죽해서 향신료와 함께 공 모양으로 요리한 쿱바(Kubbe)가 메인요리이며, 남부지방에서는 키슈나(Kishnah)가 제공된다. 요르단 남쪽 마안 지방에서는 루질 하미드(rujil hamid), 중부 지역에서는 만사프(Mansaf)를 주로 먹는데, 말린 요거트에 양고기를 넣고 납작한 빵에 양념한 밥과 함께 제공된다. 특히 만사프는 명절, 친지나 친구 방문, 약혼, 결혼식과 같은 특별한 가족 행사에 항상 차려지는 음식이다.

〈그림7〉 요르단의 결혼예복

〈그림8〉 요르단의 전통요리 만사프

Ⅲ. 오늘날의 요르단 결혼 문화

오늘날 요르단은 높은 빈곤율과 실업률, 사회적 변화로 인해 청년들의 결혼 비율이 감소하고 있다. 과거에는 요르단 청년이 27세에 결혼하면 늦었다고 여겨졌지만, 요즘은 30대에 하는 것이 일반적이다. 교육 수준 향상과 소셜 미디어로 인해 결혼에 대한 청년들의 인식 역시 크게 바뀌었다. 높은 실업률과 취업 지연을 고려하면 요르단 청년들에게는 재정 상황 개선이 가장 중요한 우선순위 중 하나가 됐다. 코로나 팬데믹 이후 결혼식장 폐쇄와 공공 집회 금지 등으로 인해 값비싼 전통 결혼식을 치르지 않고 적은 비용으로 결혼을 할 수 있게 됐지만, 30%에 달하는 실업률과 낮은 임금, 과도한 혼납금으로 인해 여전히 요르단 젊은이들은 결혼을 주저하고 있다.

현재 요르단의 월평균 임금은 586달러인 반면 요르단의 평균 결혼 비용은 14,000달러이다. 낮은 임금과 높은 결혼 비용의 격차로 많은 청년이 결혼을 주저하고 있다. 다만 지난 2013년 요르단으로 시리아 난민이 대거 유입되면서 경제적 압박과 안정에 대한 열망으로 요르단 남성과 시리아 여성 간의 결혼이 증가했다.

2022년을 기준으로 경제 상황의 악화, 높은 마흐르 비용, 물가 상승에 따른 결혼 비용 증가로 인해 요르단에는 100만여 명의 독신 여성이 있다. 1979년부터 지금까지 요르단에서 기록된 공식 수치에 따르면 결혼하지 않은 30세 이상의 여성은 지난 40년 동안 15배나 증가했다. 남성의 평균 결혼 연령은 1979년 26세에서 2016년 31.3세로 증가했고 여성의 평균 결혼 연령 역시 1979년 21.1세에서 2016년 27세로 높아졌다. 요르단의 결혼 평균 연령이 올라가고 있을 뿐만 아니라, 결혼하지 않은 독신 여성의 수 또한 가파르게 상승하고 있다.

전문가들은 결혼 감소 요인으로 경제적, 사회적 요인과 더불어 개인 문화의 확산, 여성의 대학 진학률 상승, 결혼에 대한 두려움, 막대한 책임 등을 꼽는다. 요르단 대학의 사회학 교수인 DR. Hussein AL-Khuzaie는 2018년 기준 30세 이상 미혼 남성이 약 150,000명, 27세 이상의 미혼 여성이 약 100,000명에 이르며 요르단 미혼 인구 비율이 약 45%에 도달했다고 언급한다. Al-Khuzai는 경제 부분을 가장 큰 이유로 꼽는다. 혼납금, 자하, 약혼 및 결혼식에 드는 비용이 막대하기 때문이다. 최소 3,000 디나르(4,231달러)[3]가 들것으로 예상하는데 요르단의 월평균 임금이 416 디나르(586달러)임을 감안하면 상당히 부담되는 액수이다. 덧붙여 Al-Khuzaie는 집값 상승과 가구

---

3 요르단에서 3000디나르는 4231달러이며, 요르단의 월평균 급여는 586달러이다.

및 기타 물건에 대한 전반적인 물가 상승을 꼽았다. 여기에 의료비, 병원비, 보육 용품 가격, 교육비 등 자녀 양육비까지 더해지면 결혼에 대한 부담감은 더욱 크다. 그는 이 모든 것이 결혼에 대한 젊은이들의 두려움을 불러일으켰다고 덧붙였다.

이에 따라 요르단의 청년 세대들은 교육을 받고 경제적으로 활동하는 아내를 선호하며, 이러한 조건이 충족되지 않는다면 결혼을 지연하거나 하지 않을 것이라고 강조한다. 많은 요르단 청년은 결혼보다 차를 사고 적당한 일자리를 찾는 것에 집중한다. 덧붙여 높은 이혼율과 그에 따른 사회적 문제로 인해 상당수가 외국인과 결혼할 의향도 있다고 밝혔다.

오늘날 대부분의 젊은 남녀들은 현대적 결혼식을 선호하기에, 결혼식 전날 잔치는 생략하고 피로연 개념의 왈리마는 간단한 축하 행사로 대체하고 있다. 많은 변화에도 불구하고 일부 전통적인 세부사항은 유지되고 있으며 특히 남자 측의 비용 부담은 여전히 크다. 관습에 따라 신랑이 신혼집을 장만해야 할 뿐만 아니라, 웨딩드레스, 혼납금 등 막대한 결혼 비용까지 책임져야 하기 때문이다.

요르단 대학교 샤리아 학부의 학장인 DR. Abd al-Rahman al-Kilani는 국가가 결혼을 원하는 요르단 청년을 위해 적은 비용과 작은 공간으로 개인 주택을 마련할 수 있는 '이슬람 기금 출범'을 촉구하고 있다. 요르단 정부와 시민기관이 청년들의 결혼을 장려하고 재정적 부담을 줄여주기 위한 사회적 책임을 다해야 한다는데, 많은 이들이 뜻을 모으고 있다.

참고문헌

Haitham Sarkhan. 2014. aleurs albadawy aluruduny. https://www.folkculturebh.org/ar/
index.php?issue=26&page=article&id=489 (검색일: 2022.08.29.)

Jfranews. 2016. jahat eashirat alealawinih eashirat alhuaytat. 검색, https://jfranews.com.jo/
article/150590 (검색일 2022.09.01.)

Geoffrey F. Hughes. 2021. Kinship, Islam, and the Politics of Marriage in jordan: Affection
and Mercy. Indiana University Press.

Laura Perdew. 2020. Understanding Jordan Today, Mitchell Lane.

Nadine Ajaka. 2014. Waiting longer to marry in Jordan, Aljazeera. 2022.08.19.

https://www.aljazeera.com/news/2014/5/2/waiting-longer-to-marry-in-jordan (검색일
2022.08.20.)

Roya News. 2019. Polygamy is 'uncommon' in Jordan. 2019.05.12. 검색, https://en.royanews.
tv/news/17561/Study-Polygamy-is-uncommon-in-Jordan (검색일 2022.08.20.)

Sahar Esfandiari. 2017. How to Survive a Jordanian Wedding. https://theculturetrip.com/mid-
dle-east/jordan/articles/how-to-survive-a-jordanian-wedding/ (검색일: 2022.08.29.)

Talaatieh. Jordan Culture Tradition Jaha. 검색, https://talaatieh.weebly.com/jordan-cul-
ture-tradition-jaha.html (검색일 2022.09.01.)

The Jordaninan National commission for women. 2016. mueadal almahawr bilmuhafazat
'aelaa minhu fil aleasimati. 2016.12.18. 검색, https://women.jo/ar/node/6888 (검
색일 2022.08.19.)

윤용수. 2006. 이슬람의 결혼관행. 한국이슬람학회 논총. 16(1). pp. 101-120.

사진출처

〈그림 1〉 https://talaatieh.weebly.com/jordan-culture-tradition-jaha.html (검색일 2022.09.01.)

〈그림 2〉 https://jfranews.com.jo/article/150590 (검색일 2022.09.01.)

〈그림 3〉 https://theculturetrip.com/middle-east/jordan/articles/how-to-survive-a-jor-
danian-wedding/ (검색일: 2022.08.29.)

<그림 4> https://www.folkculturebh.org/ar/index.php?issue=26&page=article&id=489 (
검색일:2022.08.29.)

<그림 5> https://eservices.sjd.gov.jo/zawajweb (검색일: 2022.09.02.)

<그림 6> https://khazaaen.org/ar/node/1397 (검색일: 2022.09.02.)

<그림 7> https://www.almadenahnews.com/article/ (검색일 2022.09.03.)

<그림 8> https://www.dimasharif.com/recipes/bedouin-jordanian-mansaf/ (검색일 2022.09.03.)

4부

튀르키예의 결혼 문화[1]
(Turkish Marriage Culture)

양민지
(부산외대 지중해지역원)

1 본 글은 양민지(2014), 『터키 동부 흑해 트라브존 지역의 신랑 매달기 풍습에 관한 연구』, 인문학연구, no.48, pp. 259-288 의 내용을 수정, 발전시켜 작성한 것임.

I. 튀르크 문화와 튀르키예

사람이 태어나서 죽기까지 반드시 거치는 인간의 성장 과정 중에서 그 사회의 지역적 특징, 자연환경, 민족성, 종교, 문화, 사상 등의 영향을 받아 생겨난 의식이나 의례를 통과의례라고 한다. 이러한 통과의례를 통하여 구성원들은 일정한 지위를 획득하게 되고 그에 따른 책임을 지니게 된다. 한 사회에 속한 어떠한 구성원이 특별한 시기에 들어서게 되면, 그 사회의 통과의례에서 정착된 각종의 의식과 의례 등을 일반적으로 지키려고 하며, 다른 구성원들 또한 그 구성원이 풍습과 통과의례를 준수하기를 기대한다. 그러나 크게는 시대 환경의 변화 이를테면 그 사회의 경제, 정치, 문화 등의 변화나 작게는 지역, 마을, 가족 내의 변화 등으로 인하여 사회가 일반적으로 정한 통과의례준칙이나 풍습 등은 사회 구성원이 행하는 실제의 관례와는 차이를 보이게 된다. 또한, 이러한 변화들이 모여 또 다른 통과의례의 모습이 정착되는 것이다.

결혼의례는 이러한 변화요소들이 매우 높은 의례 중 하나이다. 결혼의례 외에 출생의례, 성년례(관례), 상장례 등은 대체로 그 사회의 기성세대에 의해 진행이 된다고 볼 수 있다. 일례로 아이가 태어나면 아이의 부모가 아이의 건강과 성장을 위해 혹은 아이의 탄생 축하를 위해 여러 민속행위와 의례를 행한다. 상장례 또한, 부모님께서 돌아가시면 자식들이 고인에 대해 공경과 예를 표하고 애도의 목적으로 전통에 의거하여 경건하게 치르는 것이 보통이다. 출생의례는 그 대상이 아이가 중심이지만 실제 행위자는 아이의 부모이다. 또한, 상장례의 행위자는 자식들이지만 고인을 중심으로 예를 표하는 것이 목적이므로 돌아가신 부모님(혹은 어른)께 그 무게가 실린다. 그러나 결혼의례는 과거 집안끼리의 결합이라는 의식에서 출발하여 부모님의 의견과 가풍, 지역 문화적인 특징이 가장 크게 작용하였지만 근래에 들어서는 혼인 당사자들 간의 약속과 합의가 결혼의례에서 차지하는 비율이 높아지고 있다. 결혼의례는 전통의 변용과 새 문화의 흡수가 (일반적으로) 가장 쉽고 빠르다고 여겨지는 젊은이가 의례의 행위자 임과 동시에 의례의 목적 또한 두 남녀에게 초점이 맞춰지고 있다. 의례의 주도권이 부모님을 비롯한 기성세대에서 신랑 신부 즉 젊은 세대로 옮겨지고 있으며, 의례의 행위자임과 동시에 행위 목적의 대상자가 동일하다는 측면에서 결혼의례는 많은 변화를 거치고 있는 것이다. 이러한 변화는 튀르키예의 경우도 예외는 아니다. 이러한 사회적인 변화를 맞이하고 있는 가운데, 전통의례와 이와 관련된 풍습에 대한 연구는 문화적 가치뿐만 아니라 민속학적 가치를 보존할 수 있을 것이라 생각된다.

중앙아시아를 중심으로 시베리아에서 발칸반도에 이르는 광대한 지역에 퍼져 거주하고 튀르크어파를 모어로 하는 민족을 튀르크 제족이라 칭한다. 튀르키예, 카자흐스탄, 우즈베키스탄, 아제르바이잔, 키르기스스탄, 튀르크메니스탄, 러시아내 공화국인 알타이 공화국, 바슈코르토스탄, 추바시야, 하카시아, 사하 공화국, 타타르족, 투바 공화국과 몰도바 가가우지아 자치구, 우크라이나 크리미아 자치구, 중국 위구르 자치구, 북키프로스 등에 튀르크족이 거주하고 있다. 간단히 말하면 이는 현재 중앙아시아인 구소련 연방이었던 거의 대부분 나라에서 발칸반도에 이르는 지역이다. 두 번째는 튀르크 민족 언어의 다양성이다. 구소련 시절 공식언어였던 러시아를 제외해도 현재, 각 튀르크족이 사용하는 언어는 매우 다양하다. 이는 터키어, 카자흐어, 우즈벡어, 키르기즈어, 아제르바이잔어, 투크멘어, 타직어, 우크라이나어, 위구르어 등으로 계통적 측면에서 튀르크어파라고 할지라도 서로 다른 갈래로 분파되었기 때문에 사실상 상이한 언어라고 봐야 한다. 앞서 언급했다시피, 튀르크 민족은 일반적으로 무슬림이라는 공통점이 있으나, 지역적(지리적), 정치적, 사회적인 차이점으로 인해 문화가 다양하게 나타난다. 또한, 아나톨리아 반도에 위치한 튀르키예 내에도 튀르크계인(튀르키예 튀르크인, 중앙아시아 튀르크인, 아제르바이잔 튀르크인 등) 뿐 만이 아니라 쿠르드인, 조지아인, 포막인,[2] 보스니아인, 체르케스인, 아랍인, 알바니아인, 라즈인, 헴심인(아르메니아계), 유대인, 아르메니아인, 시리아인 등이 거주하고 있다. 이렇듯 다민족 국가인 튀르키예에서는 튀르크 문화뿐 만이 아니라, 여러 민족의 문화가 서로 영향을 주고 받으며 변형을 이뤘다.

Ⅱ. 튀르키예의 결혼 전통과 문화

이슬람은 거의 모든 튀르크 민족에게 광범위하게 흡수되었고, 그들의 생활문화, 정신문화에 지대한 영향을 미쳤다. 기존의 토테미즘, 애니미즘, 샤머

---

2 포막인(Pomaks): 오스만 제국의 통치 때 이슬람교로 개종한 슬라브인.

니즘, 조로아스터교, 마니교, 불교, 기독교 및 유대교 등을 흡수하여 발전시켰기 때문에 무슬림 수가 국민의 대다수인 튀르키예에서도 전통신앙과 관련된 (혹은 변형된) 민속행위들의 명맥이 희미하게나마 유지되고 있다. 튀르크의 전통신앙이었던, 조상령 숭배, 하늘신(텡그리) 숭배, 자연물숭배, 영혼 숭배, 가신(家神) 숭배, 우마이(umay)[3] 숭배, 수신(水神) 및 지신(地神) 숭배 등의 다양한 민간신앙들은 기복신앙을 바탕으로 하여, 그들의 출생의례, 성년례, 결혼의례와 상장례 가운데 아직도 그 흔적을 찾아볼 수 있다. 또한, 정통 이슬람 신앙에서는 찾아볼 수 없는 조상령과 영혼숭배와 관련된 성묘풍습, 고수레, 액막이와 벽사(辟邪)를 목적으로 소금, 물, 철 등을 이용하는 점, 흉안(凶眼)과 관련된 민속행위, 신목(神木)에 소원을 비는 종이나 천을 묶는 것, 무당(박스 혹은 박쉬 baksı) 등을 그 일례로 들 수 있다. 튀르키예인들의 민속행위는 기복(祈福), 액막이와 벽사 그리고 유희를 위한 목적 등으로 행해졌다.

  결혼은 여성과 남성이 한 개인으로 사회의 가장 기초 단위인 가정을 이루는 과정이다. 튀르키예에서의 결혼은 개인과 개인의 사회·경제적 결합을 통해 두 집안이 하나로 연결되는 중요한 통과의례 중 하나로 생각되고 있다. 현대 튀르키예인의 결혼의례는 최근 강화되고 있는 이슬람의 영향과 서구화를 이유로 튀르크 전통의 모습이 거의 사라졌고, 현대화를 거치면서 그 절차 또한 간소화되었다. 신랑과 신부의 의상, 결혼식을 치르는 곳, 하객에게 대접하는 음식 등 형식적 측면에서 많은 변화를 겪었으나, 몇몇 결혼의례 절차에서는 아직 민간 신앙적 요소 및 이와 관련된 행위를 찾아볼 수 있다. 튀르키예의 전통적 혼인 형태는 부모님의 의사에 따라 결혼을 하는 형태였으나, 현대

---

3 아이, 여자, 임산부, 산모를 보호하고 출생을 관장하는 여신 혹은 보호령의 일종.

에 들어서는 결혼 당사자들의 의견을 중심으로 결혼을 하고 있다.

튀르키예의 혼인 형태는 대부분 여자의 대낙혼(代諾婚)[4]인 부권혼(父權婚)이 높게 차지하며 근래에 들어서는 결혼 당사자인 여자와 남자의 의견이 크게 작용하고 있다. 또한, 튀르키예에는 족외혼의 한 형태인 '크즈 카츠르마(Kız Kaçırma, 처녀 훔쳐오기)'라고 불리는 약탈혼/납치혼이 나타나는데, (부계 중심) 부족사회시대부터 등장해 아직도 아나톨리아 동부지역을 비롯한 시골에서 종종 그 사례를 찾아볼 수 있다. 아나톨리아 반도 동부 혹은 동남부 지역이나 시골에서 결혼을 목적으로 남자가 여자를 납치해 올 때 여자의 의사를 무시하고, 암묵적인 합의가 전혀 없이 없이 여자를 데려오거나 생면부지의 여자를 데려와 강제로 결혼을 진행시키는 풍습이 있다. 이를 '크즈 카츠르마'라고 한다. 이와 비슷한 형태로 남자가 교제하고 있는 여자와 서로 암묵적인 합의를 하여 함께 도망가는 것을 '우이마 (uyma)' 혹은 '카츠마 (kaçma, 도망)'라고 부른다. 예를 들어, 여성과 남성이 서로 결혼의사에 합의 했으나 교제하는 여자의 집에서 반대를 할 경우, 교제하는 여자에게 여자의 의사와 반하여 집에서(부모님이) 정해준 정혼자(약혼자)가 있는 경우, 결혼식 비용을 지불할 능력이 없을 경우, 신부대[5]를 지불할 능력이 없을 경우에 이 같은 행위가 나타난다.

---

4 신부 될 여자의 아버지 혹은 남자형제의 의사와 신랑 당사자와 그의 부모의 의사에 의하여 성립되는 혼인 형태.

5 현재는 거의 찾아 볼 수 없는 사장된 풍습이다.

크즈 바크마(Kız Bakma)

　전통혼례의 형태는 중매혼이 대부분 이었으나, 현재에도 소개를 통해 만나 교제를 하고 결혼하는 경우가 많다. 전통적인 중매혼에서 보이는 결혼의 례는 남자 측에서 신부가 될 처녀를 알아보는 것으로 시작이 된다. 이 과정은 크즈 바크마 즉, 처녀 찾기, 처녀 보기라고 불린다.[6] 주변 친척이나 이웃, 지인들 가운데에서 아들과 결혼 할 만한 적당한 처녀가 있는지 보고 여성의 나이, 외모, 신체적 특징, 성격, 품행, 평판, 걸음걸이, 음식 솜씨, 가사 능력, 경제력, 교육수준, 가정환경, 신앙심 등을 알아본다. 터키어에는 여성의 외형보다 품행과 내면의 중요성에 그 가치를 두어 '*(외형의) 아름다움은 40일을 넘기지 못하고 싫증이 나지만 내면의 아름다움은 평생을 가도 질리지 않는다*'라는 말이 생겨나기도 했다. 그러나 품행이나 내면은 짧은 시간 내에 파악될 수 있는 것이 아니므로 신중히 주변인들의 평가나 의견을 물어 신붓감 후보가 결정되었다. 또한, 키나 외모, 몸의 건강상태나 결점(흠)등도 신부뿐만 아니라 적합한 신랑자리를 평가하는 요소 중의 하나였다. 결혼 당사자의 조건들뿐만 아니라 부모의 경제력, 능력, 평판, 도덕성, 신앙심 또한 중요한 고려대상이다. 조건에 부합한 여자가 있으면, 남자 측 가족 및 친척을 비롯한 여성 지인들 즉, 어머니, 이모, 고모, 형수, 이웃들이 여성의 집에 방문한다. 여성의 집에 가면 신붓감 여성은 손님들의 손에 입을 맞추며 예를 표하고 그동안 남자 측 방문객은 여성의 손님접대 품행과 신체적 특징 등을 파악하려 한다. 여성은 손님을 맞이하고 음료나 디저트 등을 접대할 때를 제외하고는 방에 들어가 있다. 신붓감이 마음에 들면 남자 측 방문객 중에 가장 나이가 많은 여

6　크즈 아라마(Kız Arama), 크즈 쏘루슈투르마(Kız Soruşturma) 등으로도 불린다.

성이 신부 측 여성 어른에게 (대체적으로 어머니) 딸이 마음에 드니 청혼을 하러 수일 내로 다시 와도 되겠느냐고 의향을 묻는다. 여성 측에서는 대부분 감사하다 전하고 남편을 비롯한 (남자)어른들께 여쭤 보겠노라고 답변한다.

크즈 이스테메(Kız İsteme)

다음은 청혼의 절차로 신랑측 아버지, 할아버지, 삼촌 그리고 이웃들이나 지인들이 여자 측 집으로 가서 혼인의 의사가 있는지 물어보는 단계인 크즈 이스테메, 청혼이다. 손님이 오면 여성 측에서는 커피나 음료를 대접한다. 근래에는 청혼을 하러 갈 때 보통 초콜릿, 로쿰 등의 디저트와 꽃을 선물로 가져간다. 여성 측에서는 벽사의 의미로, 소금을 집안에 뿌리기도 한다. 여자가 손님들에게 대접하는 커피가 달면 긍정적인 답변을 할 거라고 남자 측 손님들이 기대한다. 때에 따라서 소금을 넣어 매우 짜게 커피를 끓여오면 부정적인 답변을 할 거라고 생각되기도 한다. 그러나 여성이 남자의 인내심을 시험하기 위해 소금을 넣은 커피를 대접하여 그 남자가 끝까지 다 마시는지를 시험하기도 한다. 남자 측에서 혼인할 의사를 물어보고 여자 측에서 이를 받아들이면 예물, 예단, 혼수(가구 및 가전), 약혼시기(날짜), 혼인신고, 신혼집 등 결혼 절차에 대해 구체적으로 의논한다. 이로써 약혼이 진행된다. 결혼할 의사가 성립되면 신랑과 신부는 친척들을 방문하여 어른들께 인사를 드리고 함께 단 디저트를 먹는다. 또한, 양가 어른들과 가족, 가까운 친척들에게 예물의 일종인 쇠즈 보흐차[7] (söz bohça)라고 불리는 선물을 주고받는데, 이는 약혼을 확실시 하기 위함이며, 약혼식과 결혼식까지 필요할 (혹은 부족한) 것

---

7 옷이나 속옷 혹은 천을 넣어 보관하기 위한 (하얀) 천으로 보자기의 일종.

들에 대한 양가의 성의 표현이라고도 간주한다. 신랑측은 신부측에게 슬리퍼, 양말, 옷, 욕실용품, 약혼식 옷, 신발, 등을 보낸다. 신부측에서는 셔츠, 넥타이, 양말 손수건 등을 넣어 보낸다. 신랑측에서 신부에게는 양말, 구두, 옷감 혹은 옷, 슬리퍼, 잠옷 등을 선물로 보낸다.

니샨(Nişan)

그다음은 니샨이라고 불리는 약혼과 이를 위한 준비과정이다. 약혼식, 예단, 예물 비용을 포함한 결혼의례는 지역이나 가풍에 따라 다른 양상을 보인다. 약혼식 준비를 하기 위해 신부는 신랑 측 여성 두세 명과 함께 나가 (보통 금으로 된) 반지, 귀걸이, 팔찌, 목걸이와 시계, 신발, 슬리퍼, 가방, 속옷, 화장품 등을 사는데, 이때의 비용은 신랑측에서 댄다. 약혼식과 약혼 후에 입을 옷 등도 이때 장만을 한다. 대부분 약혼식 준비와 비용은 여성 측에서 담당하며, 약혼식은 여성의 집에서 하는 경우가 많다. 근래에 들어서 대도시에서는 호텔이나 예식장 등에서 약혼식을 하기도 한다. 신부측에서는 신랑에게 반지와 양복을 사준다. 약혼 하루 전날 신랑은 신부 측에 신부가 입을 약혼식 복과 로쿰, 차, 설탕, 커피, 콜로냐와 초콜릿 등을 보낸다. 약혼식은 보통 오후나 저녁때 하는 것이 보통이며, 약혼식 당일에는 신부는 미용실에 가서 화장과 머리를 하는데, 치장이 다 끝나고 신붓집으로 오면 신랑의 어머니 혹은 가장 가까운 친척 중 한 명이 일전에 신부를 위해 구매했던 액세서리를 신부에게 달아준다. 그런 후에 신부는 어른들께 손에 입을 맞추며 감사와 예를 표시하고, 신부 측에서는 신랑 측이 가져온 셔벗, 차, 로쿰 등을 대접한다. 또한, 신랑과 신부는 약혼반지를 나눠 낀다. 약혼 동안 몇 차례씩 신랑측과 신부측은 디저트와 선물 등을 가지고 서로를 방문하고, 방문객들을 위해 정성스

레 음식을 장만하여 대접한다. 지역에 따라 신부측에서 신랑측으로 혹은 신랑측에서 신부측으로 단 디저트를 보내거나 밥과 고기 등을 보내기도 한다. 약혼 기간은 당사자들의 상황 즉 학업, 군대, 직장, 건강 등의 문제를 고려하여 길어지기도 한다. 보통 6개월에서 1년 정도의 약혼 기간을 두는 것이 일반적이다. 예전에는 파혼을 할 경우 이를 부정적으로 보는 시선이 적지않게 있었으나, 현대에는 그렇지 않다. 서로의 뜻이 맞지 않을 경우나 양가에서 결혼이 적합하지 않다고 느낄 경우 등에 종종 파혼을 한다. 부모의 동이 없이 구두로 당사자들끼리 만 결혼을 약속하는 것과 양가 부모님의 허락을 받고 약혼식을 하는 경우는 엄밀히 구분을 두어 밝히고 있다.

결혼식과 과정은 크게 두 과정으로 나뉘는데 크나 게제씨(Kına Gecesi, 헤나의 밤)와 결혼식 당일에 치르는 의례이다. 결혼식 전에 신부측에서 체

〈그림 1〉 약혼식, 신랑의 아버지가 신부에게 반지를 끼워주는 모습

이즈(çeyiz, 혼수로 해오는 가정용품의 일종)[8]를 보내오는데 신랑 측에서는 이를 이웃들과 친척들에게 보여주는데, 이는 아나톨리아 내륙지방에서 흔히 볼 수 있는 전통적 행위이다.[9] 자수를 새긴 침실용품 및 장식장 깔개, 가전제품 덮개, 컵 받침, 손뜨개로 만든 욕실용품, 수건, 숄, 아기 옷, 머리쓰개 등의 수제품이 이에 해당한다. 또한, 침구류와 속옷, 의류, 카펫, 청동으로 만들어진 주방 냄비와 쟁반, 솥 등도 체이즈에 포함되며 근래에 들어서는 신부 측 가정형편에 따라 가전제품 등도 포함된다. 신부 측에서 신랑 측으로 체이즈를 보낼 때, 산득(Sandık)이라고 불리는 큰 함에 넣어 보낸다. 이때 신부 측 함지기가 함 위에 앉아 신랑 측에게 돈을 요구하기도 하며, 신랑 측에서는 함지기와 흥정을 하고 체이즈를 받는다. 투르크멘인들도 이와 비슷하게 혼수를 보여주는 전통행위가 있다. 결혼식 당일 아침 신부 측에서 준비한 혼수를 신랑 측에서 몇 사람이 신부의 집을 방문해 신랑 측 집으로 가져가는데, 이때 신랑 측에서는 혼수를 준비해 준 신부측에 모든 예를 갖추어 고마움을 표한다. 신랑 측에서 온 사람은 혼수를 가져가 는 길에 마을 사람이 이를 볼 수 있도록 동네를 행진한다.

또한, 지역에 따라서 신부 측 친구와 친척들을 신랑측에서 하맘 (hamam, 목욕탕)에 초대를 한다. 신부와 신부측 손님들은 신랑측 여성들과 함께 노래를 부르고 음료도 즐기며 일종의 정화의식을 행한다. 겔린(gelin, 신부) 하맘[10] 이라고 불리는 이 정화의식 후에는 신랑측에서 쌀로 만든 수프, 안에

---

8   손뜨개로 만든 욕실용품, 침실용품, 자수를 놓아 새긴 수건, 장식장 깔개, 가전제품 덮개, 컵 받침, 숄, 아기 옷 등의 (수)제품을 일컬음.

9   딸을 가진 어머니는 아이가 어릴 때부터 틈틈이 준비해 놓는다.

10   요즈갓(Yozgat)과 씨바스(Sivas) 지역에서는 신랑과 신랑 친구들이 귀베이 하마므(Güvey Hamanı, 신랑 목욕)를 즐긴다.

쌀과 고기, 채소 등을 채워 만든 음식의 일종인 돌마 (dolma), 아슈레(Aşure, 디저트의 일종)[11]등을 대접한다. 이 정화의식은 신부 및 신부측 지인과 신랑 측 여성 간의 친목을 도모하는 것으로, 투르크 전통 신앙인 물 숭배 사상에서 기원한 풍습으로 볼 수 있다.

크나 게제씨(Kına Gecesi, 헤나의 밤)

결혼식 전날 밤에는 크나 게제씨를 치르는데, 이는 신부의 집에서 행해지는 결혼의례의 하나이다. 전통적으로 크나 게제씨는 신붓집에서 이뤄지지만 근래에 들어서는 특별한 장소(회관, 학교 등)를 빌려 하기도 한다. 크나 게제씨에 온 여성 들은 구슬픈 민요를 함께 불러 신부의 눈물샘을 자아내게 한다. 이는 신붓집에 신부의 가족, 친구, 친인척, 이웃 지인 등이 한자리에 모여 신부를 떠나보내는 아쉬움과 슬픔 등을 나누고 동시에 결혼을 축복해 주는 여성의 의례이다. 신부는 헤나 의식이 끝날 때까지 빨간색 천으로 만들어진 베일로 얼굴을 가린다. 결혼의례에서 빨간색이 자주 이용되는 것은, 전통적으로 악귀들이 빨간색을 무서워하기 때문에 이를 사용하면 잡귀나 액운을 물리칠 수 있다고 믿어져 왔기 때문이다. 크나 게제씨는 신부와 신랑의 손바닥에 동전[12]을 올려놓고 그 주위와 손가락을 헤나로 물을 들이는 행위에서 이름이 붙여졌다. 여성들이 헤나가 올려진 쟁반 위의 촛불에 불을 붙여 가져오

---

11 이슬람력의 첫 번째 달 이름(정월)인 무하람 10일째인 아슈레 귀뉘(Aşure Günü, 아슈레 명절) 에 만들어 먹는 디저트이다. 노아가 대홍수 이후 육지에 처음으로 발을 내디뎠을 때 방주에 있던 재료로 만들었다고 믿는 음식(디저트)이다. 전통적으로 최소 7가지의 재료, 혹은 10가지의 재료로 만들어지는데, 물, 밀, 우유, 설탕, 콩, 쌀, 병아리콩, 말린 과일(건포도, 건살구, 건무화과 등), 견 과류, 등이 그것이다. 호두, 계피, 석류, 코코넛 가루 등을 고명으로 얹어 먹는다.

12 예전에는 금화나 은화 등을 사용했으며, 이때 사용한 동전은 액운을 물리쳐 준다고 믿어 평생 잘 보관했다.

면, 남편이 살아있거나 이혼하지 않은 여성 즉, 남편과의 금실이 좋은 여성이 신랑과 신부의 손에 헤나로 물을 들여준다. 헤나 물을 들이면 진한 빨간색이 나타나는데, 앞서 말한 것처럼 붉은색의 주술적인 기능을 믿는 데에서 헤나를 사용하는 것이다. 헤나의식이 끝나면 함께 연주단의 연주에 맞춰 춤을 추고 노래를 부르며 즐긴다. 전통 혼례식에서 신부는 신랑이 보낸 말 혹은 마차를 타고 신랑집으로 가서 혼례를 치렀으나, 현대 대도시에서는 보통 차를 타고 예식장(혹은 신랑집)으로 이동을 한다. 이때 집을 나서는 신부에게 신부 아버지는 빨간색 천으로 만든 허리띠를 세 번 감아주며, 이는 벽사의 의미와 함께 신부의 순결함을 나타내는 것이다. 튀르키예 전통 결혼의례에서는 크나 게제씨 다음 날 아침에 신랑 측에서 신부를 신랑집으로 데려가는 겔린 알라이으(Gelin Alayı, 신부맞이 일행)가 신붓집에 오며, 예전에는 말에 태워 신부를 데려왔으나, 근래 시골에는 자동차나 미니버스, 승합차 등이 이용되기도 한다. 신부맞이 일행에는 보통 신랑의 형수, 누나, 동생 등 여성들이 신부를 돕기 위해 참여하며 신랑의 아버지와 결혼의례를 담당하는 어른들이 함께 온다. 그러나 신랑의 어머니는 참여하지 않는 것이 보통이다. 겔린 알라이는 신랑집에서 북과 나팔을 불며 신부를 데리러 신붓집으로 온다. 그동안 신랑 측에서는 신부를 맞이할 준비를 한다. 신부는 신랑 측 일행이 도착하면 방에서 나오는데, 이때에는 아버지와 형제들이 신부를 도와 데리고 나온다. 신부맞이 일행이 신붓집을 나서면 신부 측 동네 젊은이들이 앞을 막고 못 가게 하는 경우도 있으며, 신랑 측에서는 이들에게 무엇을 원하느냐 묻고 그에 상응하는 소정의 돈이나 대가를 지급한다. 신랑집과 신붓집에서는 신부의 순탄한 시댁 생활을 기원하고 행복한 결혼생활과 제액초복을 위한 여러 행위를 한다. 신부를 데리고 온 일행이 신랑집에 도착할 거라는 소식을 제일 먼저 전하는 이 에게는 신랑의 어머니가 일정의 돈 혹은 비단 옷감을 건네기도 한다. 신부맞이 일행이 신랑집에 당도하면 신랑의 남자 형제의 부인 (형수나 사촌 형수 등)과 혼인의례를 주재하는 어른이 함께 신부가 타고 온 수단에서 신부를 내린다. 신부를 내리기 전과 내린 후 그리고 집에 들어서기까지 여러 민속의례가 행해지는데 이는 첫째로 신부가 시댁에 복을 가져다 주기를 바라는 마음에서, 둘째로 시댁에 잘 적응하여 모두가 평안해지길 바라는 마음에서, 셋째로 후손을 바라고 건강을 기원하는 마음에서 이뤄졌다.

〈그림 2〉 크나게제씨

〈그림 3〉 크나게제씨 신부의 손 물들이는 과정

특히, 신부가 신랑집에 들어갈 때, 복과 다산을 기원하는 의미로 신랑측 하객은 신부의 머리에 견과류, 작은 사탕, 밀알, 수수 등을 던진다. 터키어로 수수는 'Darı'라고 하는데, 이러한 풍습 때문에 미혼의 남성이나 여성에게 '당신에게도 곧 좋은 일이 일어나기를 바랍니다.'라는 의미로 '다르쓰 바쉬느자!'(Darısı başınıza!) 라는 축언을 한다.

니캬(Nikah)

니캬는 결혼을 의미하는데, 이는 혼인신고와 증명을 위한 절차를 나타내기도 한다. 대부분 결혼식 전에 하거나 결혼식의 한 순서로 진행한다. 니캬는 남녀가 증인 2명 앞에서 서로 부부가 될 것을 동의하고 주례가 성혼을 선포하는 절차이다. 니캬는 정부가 인정하는 행정법적인 것과 이슬람 율법에 따른 종교적 니캬(Dinî Nikah)[13]로 나뉜다. 튀르키예 정부에서는 행정법상의 니캬 만을 인정 하고 있다. 행정법상의 니캬를 거치면 주민등록상에 기혼으로 표기가 된다. 행정법상의 니캬뿐만이 아니라 대다수가 무슬림인 튀르키예인에게는 종교적 니캬도 매우 중요하게 생각되고 있다. 일부에서는 종교적 니캬만을 치르고 하나 이상의 부인을 두는 경우도 있다. 그러나 이는 불법이다. 공식적인 니캬는 시청 결혼의례 담당 공무원이 주례를 보며, 결혼식처럼 성대하게 혹은 간단하게 절차만 밟기도 한다. 종교적인 니캬는 이맘(İmam)이 주례를 보며, 무슬림 남성 증인 2명을 대동한다.

---

13 이맘 니캬흐(İmam Nikahı)라고도 불린다.

결혼식(Düğün)

결혼 예식에서는 주례가 없으며, 보통 공식적인 니캬 의례를 결혼식과 함께한다. 결혼 서약과 성혼발표가 끝나면 하객들에게 음식과 음료를 대접하거나 간단한 식음료와 다과만을 대접하는 경우도 있다. 연주단의 연주에 맞춰 하객, 친척, 신랑 신부가 춤을 추고 즐기고 나면, 하객들은 신랑 신부에게 축의금을 준다. 신부는 빨간 천으로 만든 띠를 어깨에서 허리까지 대각선으로 매단다. 하객들은 신부의 붉은 띠에 준비해온 금목걸이, 금팔찌 등의 액세서리나 금으로 만들어진 동전, 돈 등을 달아준다. 결혼의례를 치르며 신부는 많은 축하품과 돈을 받는 데, 특히 크나 게제씨, 니샨, 결혼식에서는 시부모와 중매인, 신랑 측 지인들로부터 금목걸이, 금반지, 금팔찌, 시계 등을 받는다. 하객들의 방문과 성의 표시에 신랑 신부는 감사의 의미로 전통인사를 드리거나 포옹을 한다. 보통 결혼식은 뒤윈 살롱(Düğün Salon, 결혼식장)에서 하지만, 시골이나 경제적 사정이 좋지 못하면 집 근처 공터나 아파트 입구 등에서 하기도 한다. 공식적인 결혼 혹은 종교적 결혼 이후 신부와 신랑이 함께하는 것을 게르덱 (Gerdek)이라고 하는데, 니캬 후 신랑과 신부가 함께 머무는 신방을 게르덱 에비(Gerdek Evi)[14]라고 부른다. 신랑은 신방에 들어가기 전 복을 비는 간단한 기도를 하거나 독실한 무슬림일 경우 예배를 드리기도 한다. 경험 많은 여성 연장자(형수 혹은 사촌 형수)가 신랑과 신부의 손을 맞잡게 하고 신방에서 나오는데, 지방에 따라서는 간단한 음료를 가져다주는 경우도 있으며, 이날의 수고에 대한 사례를 받기도 한다. 튀르키예에서는 신랑과 신부가 부부로서 인정받는 이 첫날밤을 게르덱 게제씨(Gerdek

---

14 게르덱 오다쓰(Gerdek Odası), 게르덱 다므(Gerdek Damı) 등으로도 불린다.

Gecesi), 혹은 지파프 게제씨(Zifaf Gecesi)라고 부른다. 전통 결혼식에선 신랑집에 차려진 게르덱 에비에서 신혼 첫날밤을 보냈으나, 최근 대도시에서는 호텔에서 보내는 것이 대부분이다. 요즘에는 결혼식이 끝나면 신랑 신부는 신혼여행을 가며, 신혼여행에서 돌아오면 신랑 측 지인이나 친척, 이웃이 신부를 보러 신랑집(혹은 신혼집)에 모인다. 이는 전통 결혼의례에서 기인한 것으로 예전에는 혼례 다음날 신부를 보기 위해 여성 이웃과 여성 지인이 아침 일찍 방문하여 정오까지 먹고 마시며 결혼을 축하했다. 저녁 시간에는 남성들이 모여 즐기는데, 여성들은 자리를 따로 했다. 요새는 신부를 보기 위해 방문한 이들에게 간단하게 커피, 차, 로쿰, 견과류 등의 디저트나 다과를 대접하며 이러한 방문은 며칠 동안이나 계속된다.

Ⅲ. 시간과 공간의 변화 속에서 문명의 교류를 담고 있는 결혼

특정 지역의 문화는 그 문화를 발생시키고 영위하는 사회 구성원들과 같은 인적 환경, 문화의 토대와 배경이 되는 자연적 환경 그리고 역사나 종교와 같은 사회적 환경에 따라 변화한다. 튀르키예는 아나톨리아 반도에 있으며, 북쪽으로 흑해, 서쪽으로 에게해, 남쪽으로는 지중해를 접하고 있다. 또한, 북동쪽에는 카프카스와 남동쪽에는 이란고원이 위치 해 있다. 국경을 접한 나라로는 북동쪽으로 조지아, 아르메니아, 동쪽으로 아제르바이잔, 이란, 남쪽으로 이라크와 시리아, 북서쪽으로 그리스와 불가리아가 있다. 다양한 자연환경과 천혜의 지리를 지닌 아나톨리아 반도는 예로부터 아카드, 아시리아, 히

타이트, 아르메니아, 로마, 셀주크, 오스만 제국 등과 같은 많은 제국의 문화권 아래 있었으며, 수많은 민족이 터전을 잡거나 거쳐 갔다. 이처럼 긴 역사 속에서 아나톨리아 반도에는 다양한 문화와 문명이 생성되었고 후대의 튀르키예 공화국에서도 그 영향을 미쳤다. 이 가운데 결혼의례는 지역환경과 가풍, 종교 그리고 시대 등에 따라 매우 다른 양상을 보이는 복합적인 통과의례 중 하나이다. 즉, 공간과 시간의 제약을 많이 받으며, 현재와 과거가 동시에 공존하고 있는 의례 중 하나라고 말할 수 있다. 결혼식 자체만을 보면 매우 현대적으로 변하여 전통적인 요소나 민속 행위들을 거의 찾아볼 수 없지만, 결혼을 준비하기까지의 과정과 결혼 이후 일련의 행위들을 관찰하다 보면 그 속에 전통적 요소들이 내재되어 있음을 발견할 수 있다.

〈그림 4〉 튀르키예 결혼식

〈그림 5〉 튀르키예 결혼식

〈그림 6〉 튀르키예 결혼식, 하객이 신랑에게 축의금을 걸어주고 있다.

〈그림 7〉 튀르키예 결혼식 하객들이 축의금으로 걸어 준 돈, 금
액세서리를 하고 있는 신랑과 신부

참고문헌

Erman Artun. *Türk Halkbilimi*. Kitabevi, İstanbul, 2005.

Pertev Naili Boratav. *100 soruda Türk Halkedebiyatı*. Gerçek Yayınları, İstanbul, 1969.

Çetin Cengiz. "Türk Düğün Gelenekleri ve Kutsal Evlilik Ritüeli". Ankara Üniversitesi Dil ve Tarih-Coğrafya

Fakültesi Dergisi, S48, Ankara, 2008, 111-121p,

Nermin Erdentuğ. "Türkiye'nin Karadeniz Bölgesinde evlenme görenekleri ve törenleri". Ankara Üniversitesi

Dil ve Tarih Coğrafya Fakültesi Antropoloji Dergisi, S.4, Ankara, 1967, 27-64p.

_____ "Türkiye'nin Karadeniz Bölgesinde evlenme görenekleri ve törenleri". Ankara Üniversitesi

Dil ve Tarih Coğrafya Fakültesi Antropoloji Dergisi, S.5, Ankara, 1969, 231-266p.

İsmaıil Görkem. "Doğu Karadeniz Bölgelsi Düğünlerinde Görülen Enişteyi Tavana Asma Geleneği".

Uluslararası Trabzon ve Çevresi Tarih ve Kültür Sempozyumu Bildiri, Trabzon Türk Ocağı, 2006.

Turgut Günay. "Rize-Trabzon Yöresinde Enişteyi Tavana Asma Geleneği". Türk Folklor Araştırmaları, c. XIV, S. 283, 1973, 6560p.

Yaşar Kalafat. *Doğu Anadolu'da Eski Türk İnançlarının İzleri*. ebabil Yayınları, Ankara, 2006.

Sedat Veyis Örnek. *Türk Halkbilimi*. İş Bankası Kültür Yayınları, Ankara, 1977.

Sibel Turhan Tuna. "Türk Dünyasındaki Düğünlerde Koltuklama ve Kırmızı Kuşak Bağlama Geleneği". bilig, Yaz, 2006, S38, 149-160p.

사진 출처

〈그림 4〉 https://www.trthaber.com/haber/turkiye/hakkarideki-dugunde-geline-5-kilo-altin-damada-5-milyon lira-takildi-697036.html (검색일: 2022.09.01)

5부

이란의 결혼 문화
(Marriage Culture in Iran)

무함마드 하산 모자파리(Mozafari, Mohammad Hassan)

(부산외대 지중해지역원)

I. Introduction

Iran occupies an area of 1,648,195 square kilometers in Western Asia, making it the 17th largest country in the world by area. Because of the unique geographical location of this country, it has historically served not only as a bridge between the three continents of Asia, Europe, and Africa but has also been a meeting place for different civilizations, religions, and ethnic groups since the time of the Persian civilization. Having thousands of kilometers of common borders with the countries of the region and over 5800 square kilometers of coastline with the Caspian Sea in the north and the Persian Gulf and the Oman Sea in the south, and Eurasian countries in the north and Central Asian countries in the east, Iran enjoys a unique position. The exceptional situation has resulted in Iran being home to a variety of ethnic groups, including Persian, Baluch, Turkmen, Lur, Armenian, Azeri, Kurdish, Arab, and others. However, Persian culture remains the dominant culture in Iran. Iran is a multicultural country in which different ethnic groups have lived peacefully together for thousands of years. The cultures of these ethnic groups are often closely related to those of their neighboring countries. Due to the fact that the majority of Iranians adhere to Islam, the general culture of modern Iran is heavily influenced by Islamic teachings. It is important to note, however, that most people's celebrations and rituals, literature, art, and architecture have deep roots in their historical and national traditions. The Persian language, its various dialects and accents, national festivities such as Nowruz1 (New Year's Eve), Yalda Night (the longest night of the year) and Iranian solar calendar, philosophy and mysticism, Iranian art, particularly traditional music, Persian literature and poetry, architecture, and decorative arts, as well as the cultures of ethnic groups and Iranian cuisine, as well as the grand celebrations of weddings, comprise the most prominent elements of Islamic-Iranian culture. Therefore, marriage customs or any socio-cultural issue has a deep, wide, and colorful historical background.

A wedding is the celebration of the beginning of a life together and the formation of a family, which is the most fundamental pillar of society. From a macro perspective, the family is the leading

---

1   Nowruz is recognized by UNESCO as a cultural and spiritual heritage of humanity, and the United Nations General Assembly adopted a resolution recognizing March 21, the first day of spring, as the International Day of Nowruz. Many different religions and countries celebrate this ancient Iranian ritual.

school, the center of education and training, and the main conduit for the transfer of experiences to future generations. The success, health, and desire of a family will lead to the development of a generation that is physically, emotionally, mentally healthy, aware, law-abiding, and responsible in all aspects of life. All nations, societies, and governments place a great deal of importance on the family. It is because of the importance of the role of the family that Article 16 of a milestone document in the history of human rights, the Universal Declaration of Human Rights, not only recognized "the right to marry and to found a family", rather emphasized that "the family is the natural and fundamental group unit of society and is entitled to protection by society and the State." (United Nation Organization, 2022). In 1993, also the General Assembly decided in a resolution (A/RES/47/237) that 15 May of every year should be observed as The International Day of Families (UN Family Rights, 2022).

Iranians' national and Islamic culture has always emphasized marriage and establishing a strong and stable family relationship. Since marriage is basically a welcome step to start a family, and an honest and loving decision to start a life, wedding customs and ceremonies are held very magnificently.

II. Marriage customs

Iranians have cherished the wedding celebration with its set of religious and cultural customs since ancient times. Wedding ceremonies and customs have always been influenced by the political and social positions as well as the economic, cultural, and religious standings of the bride and groom's families. Wedding ceremonies for political, social, and religious figures and their children have a greater impact on the general public than wedding ceremonies for other classes of society and have even prompted various guilds to become actively involved. As the wedding celebration of the king and princes was a public event, the greater the social status and influence of the bride and groom's family, the greater the involvement of various guilds.

Weddings and customs were celebrated with the utmost splendor by prominent families, kings, and princes, initiating social joy and happiness among the people. Family members tried to organize ceremonies and customs in the best possible way with empathy, cooperation, and collective participation at the local and rural levels as well. The customs of the wedding ceremony, with specific names, were organized to meet a specific goal in a specific sequence according to a precise plan. These customs assist in preparing the bride and groom and their families for marriage (from the stage of getting to know one another to form a marital and independent life).

In addition to preparing the necessary facilities and equipment, the customs involved welcoming the families, procurement agents, and guests of the ceremony. In the past, the bride and groom's families, their close and distant relatives, worked together and actively participated in preparing syrup and sweets, bringing firewood, baking bread, cooking, preparing food, and serving the guests at the wedding ceremony. Some ceremonies, such as fetching firewood, baking bread, and entertaining a large number of guests were not possible without the cooperation and sympathy of relatives and friends (wedding ceremonies in Kalardasht). Additionally, the ceremony included various entertainments such as hand-to-hand matches, wrestling matches, and various performances such as dance and music.

A number of great Persian poets have written poems and stories about wedding ceremonies and the customs of kings and other people as well as lovers. Though these poems, stories, and legends and their elements and characters and what they narrated are not true, however, historically, these stories reflect the culture, social interaction, and customs of various periods. The transmission of ancient and national beliefs, values, and customs from one generation to another is considered hidden learning in anthropology. Literature, legends, and stories convey customs, ceremonies, and rituals. For example, the story of the Hesari lady in Haftpaykar by Nizami (Ganjavi, 2022), and Malek-zadeh's tale of the daughter of the King of China and her questions to suitors have well explained the ancient marriage customs of Iranians.

Fakhr al-Din Asad Gorgani, in his famous poem Divan "Weiss and Ramin", while describing the story of the wedding of Weiss,[2] an Iranian prince, with the king and Priest of Marv, and after the king's death, his marriage with Ramin (the king's brother), He has described some Iranian wedding customs and celebrations, such as determining the time of the wedding according to astrology, determining the dowry (Based on Islamic jurisprudence, it is one of the obligations in the marriage contract) and Shir-Baha from the groom to the bride, setting up a party, the bride's make-up, and also games and entertainment were part of the ceremony. The story of Weiss' wedding dates back to the pre-Islamic era.

---

2 "Weiss and Ramin" is one of the most famous romantic poems in Persian literature, describing the customs, rituals, and culture of that time period. The king of Marv was in love with Weiss, the daughter of the king of Mahabad, but the girl's family opposed such a proposal and marriage, so the king of Marv sent an army under the command of his brother Ramin to Mahabad, killing the king and defeating him, and taking the girl with him, Ramin returned to Marv. Nevertheless, Ramin fell in love with her at first sight. Weiss and Ramin, the brother of King of Marv, escaped once, and after many plots, Ramin marries Weiss. The origin of the story is related to the Parthian period.

Anyway, in short, the roots of Iranian marriage customs should be sought in this great work of Persian literature. Ferdowsi has explained numerous stories of all types of marriages within and outside the family, far and near, marriages of kings with lower classes, romantic and political marriages in his Shahnameh,[3] and in every story, many marriage customs such as Courtship, marriage, gift giving and moving the bride and groom to the new house have been beautifully expressed (Jafari, 2022).

Modern Iran is the heir to Persian history, culture, and civilization. The multilingual, cultural, religious, racial, and linguistic society of modern Iran is like an ancient mother, preserving the diverse cultures and traditions of its ancestors. Iran's marriage ceremonies and customs have deep roots in pre-Islamic (Persian culture and civilization) and post-Islamic Iranian civilization. Due to this, Iranian marriage customs are very diverse and are closely related to the culture and customs of each Iranian ethnic groups while cultural and religious developments during different historical periods have had a greater or lesser impact on these ceremonies and customs, many of these customs remain prevalent among Iranians and the

---

3   The work of Abul-Qasem Ferdowsi Tosi, with about 50,000 lines of poetry, is one of the largest and most prominent epic poems in the world. He has been working tirelessly for thirty years to create a literary masterpiece and protect the Persian language and culture. The content of the Shahnameh includes the legends, culture and history of Iran from the beginning to the Arab invasion in the 7th century AD.

ancient Persian cultural area, as well as conversions to Islam. It did not result in the removal of these customs, and most of them were not opposed by Islamic rulings.

Islam considers marriage as a desirable tradition and strongly encourages Muslims to help young people get married.[4] Marriage is referred to in the Quran as a source of peace for the human soul and a sign of God's mercy.[5] Prophet Mohammad said: Marriage is my tradition, so if someone (without reason) refuses to marry, it is not from me (Al-Jawahiri, 1981, p. 12). The family is not just a legal entity. It has different dimensions including religious, moral, and social. Many verses and hadiths have dealt with various topics about the rulings, rights, and ethics of marriage and family, for example, the importance of family, the purpose of having a family, family management, dowry, alimony, types of divorce, the rights of divorced women, the rights of children and inheritance (Arberry (translated by), 2015, p. 27). Therefore, marriage and its customs, from courtship to marriage and living together under one roof, are deeply rooted not only in the national culture but Islamic teachings too.

---

4 The Holy Quran, 24: 32 stated: "Marry the spouseless among you, and your slaves and handmaidens that are righteous; if they are poor, God will enrich them of His bounty; God is All-embracing, All-knowing." (Arberry (translated by), 2015, p. 354).

5 The Holy Quran, 30: 21 stated: "And of His signs is that He created for you, of yourselves, spouses, that you might repose in them, and He has set between you love and mercy. Surely in that are signs for a people who consider. (Arberry (translated by), 2015, p. 406).

Article 10 of the Constitution of the Islamic Republic of Iran recognizes the family as the fundamental unit of Islamic society. It stated: "Since the family is the fundamental unit of the Islamic society, all related laws and regulations and planning should facilitate the formation of the family, protect its sanctity and, family relations should be based on Islamic law and ethics" (The Constitution of the Islamic Republic of Iran, 2022). According to Article 20 of the Iranian Family Law, it is mandatory to register a marriage in the notary office. Also, it is obligatory to conclude the marriage contract according to Islamic jurisprudence (Farhange Tafahum, 2022). But customs and cultural ceremonies do not play a role in the validity of the marriage.

In the last few decades, modern culture and art, the requirements of city life, inter-ethnic marriages, new technologies, and most especially the film industry have had a significant influence on Iranian wedding ceremonies and customs. The wedding customs are being modified to accommodate the developments and requirements of the modern world as much as possible. As a result of cultural and social changes, some customs and special stages of the wedding ceremony have been removed, changed, or simplified. In the past, wedding celebrations lasted from a month to a week, but now the ceremony and customs are shorter and more compact, and the form of their customs has also changed. In recent years, some customs and traditions have become more modern and prominent and are celebrated more and more magnificently, enthusiastically, and loudly.

Since the Corona epidemic spread several years ago, extraordinary restrictions have been placed on all visits, gatherings and celebrations, even at the family level, including wedding ceremonies. As the situation improved, people returned to an almost normal life and began to gather again, including to celebrate weddings. In this article, you will be introduced to different aspects of Iranian culture, customs, marriage ceremonies, and their various stages. It is not possible to cover all the customs and stages of marriage celebration in one article due to the diversity of customs and stages in the multicultural society of Iran. As a result, we will focus on the most important phases of courtship, engagement ceremony, wedding ceremony, dowry and wedding shopping, Hanabandan ceremony, wedding ceremony, honeymoon and mother-in-law greetings which are generally found throughout Iran.

1. Courtship ceremony

Throughout history, families have always been very careful when choosing life partners for their children. If a wrong choice is made, the bride and groom as well as their families will face many problems. There has been a tremendous amount of economic, social, cultural, and political change due to urbanization, so families, even immediate family members, no longer know one another on an economic, social, cultural, or political level as they used to. For the purpose of forming a good family, finding an appropriate partner is the most important investment. In determining the fate of future generations, this choice is of critical importance. It is essential for both parties to be familiar with one another in order to have a successful marriage. Courtship meetings and initial outings provide an opportunity for boys and girls and their families to get to know one another.

In ancient Iran, it was customary for the bride's mother and sister to select a suitable bride for the groom. After consulting with him about the desired girl, they would propose to her if he agreed. Nowadays, girls and boys have access to a wide variety of spaces, conditions, and methods for getting to know one another, and some have actually proposed unofficially, without the knowledge of their families, and traditional and formal courtship ceremonies are performed once the girls and boys have decided. As a matter of fact, in the traditional matchmaking meeting, some women from the groom's family attend the bride's house in order to get a closer look at her.

During the reception, the bride and her family welcome the groom and his family and answer their questions. In the case of a positive reaction from the groom's family, they propose marriage to the girl, otherwise, they leave the parties following the customary talks and compliments. However, if both parties are in agreement, the next courtship meeting will be held in the groom's presence with the permission of the bride's parents. With flowers and sweets, the groom's family goes to the girl's house wearing formal clothes as a sign of respect and courtesy. In this meeting, girls and boys discuss their interests and get to know each other better. Following the party meeting, if the bride and groom are compatible, a gift will be given to the bride.

Generally, in Iran, the family of the boy proposes to the girl; and it is not common for women to propose to men. Traditionally, in Shahnameh stories, the groom and his family proposed marriage to the girl's family, according to the customs. As part of this important task, the elders are given the following assignment: "For the marriage of his three sons, Fereydun (an Iranian legendary king) assigns one of his nobles named Jandal to search everywhere for three sisters of the race of the elders who are "fairy-faced and pure and well-known", and after many hours of searching, he finds these characteristics in the daughters of the Shah of Yemen and proposes her. Moreover, Kay Kavus (an Iranian legendary king) sends a wise and smooth-tongued warrior to the King of Hamavaran to propose to Sudabah, whom he has only heard about her. Afrasiab's[6] daughter, Farangis, is also proposed to by Siavash (a legendary Iranian prince). In spite of the fact that all the ceremonies of the wedding of Rostam (a legendary hero in Persian mythology) and Tahmina (Rostam's wife) are performed in an unexpected manner in one night (with a sudden appearance in Rostam's house), the "artful Zoroastrian priest" performs the act of courtship.

It has sometimes been the responsibility of these men to select a bride from among the desired girls; similar to how Anoushirvan selects a wise person to choose the daughter of Khaqan Chin and instructs him to be careful not to be seduced by the appearance of the daughters. For the purpose of marrying an Indian girl, Iskandar assigns nine wise men to see the girl and, after they approve, he marries her. It is still customary in some areas of Iran for men to court women rather than for women to marry. For example, among Shahsavans in East Azerbaijan and Takab Afshar in West Azerbaijan, marriage is conducted by two elders related to the groom.

It should be noted, however, that in the past communication between men and women was not as easy as it is today, and men and women were not able to see each other easily before marriage, so

---

6   The mythical king of Turan.

boys and girls were obtaining information about one another by asking others, or in exceptional circumstances. However, if a girl fell in love with a boy's beauty, morals, and character, the girl or her family would propose marriage. This kind of courtship is beautifully and attractively expressed in famous Iranian literature, for example in Ferdowsi's Shahnameh.

On any pretext or occasion, the girls conveyed their love and interest to the boy of their choice by sending a message to the boys. There are many examples of such love in Ferdowsi's Shahnameh, all of which have led to marriage and union. There have been numerous examples of girls courting boys, including the wedding of Zal and Rudabah (father of Rostam and daughter of Mehrab Shah of Kabul), Tahmina and Rostam (father and mother of Sohrab, the daughter of the king of Samangan city), Bijan and Manijeh (son of Giv and daughter of Afrasiab), and Katayon, the daughter of Rome's king and Gashtasb (Iranian prince According to Manijeh's story) when she saw Bijan, she fell in love with him and asked her nanny to bring him to her. There are times when a girl expresses her love for a boy in an indirect manner. In order to demonstrate her worth and competence, Nemud applied make-up, wore bright colors, played music and sang, and also took the initiative in verbal communication with her preferred partner. Similarly, Shirin has made Khosrow Parviz infatuated with makeup and wearing special clothes, Mehrak Noushzad's daughter, Shapur Ardeshir, by showing her physical ability and speaking clearly, and Mahyar Goharforosh's daughter, Bahram Gur, by showing her musical talent. By these methods, they expressed their love and interest to them (Jafari, 2022, pp. 5-9).

2. Initial wedding ceremony

Following the bride's acceptance of the groom, the first ceremony is held to commemorate this event. One of the customs associated with marriage in Iran is the "Bride's saying yes" ceremony. Upon receiving a positive response from the girl's family, the yes ceremony is held. In addition to the families of the bride and groom, the elders of each party's family are also present during this ceremony. This ceremony is primarily intended to determine the amount of dowry, the type of dowry, the way of holding rituals, and the plan for the rituals. In determining the timing of ceremonies, traditional, cultural, and religious affiliations (Islamic, Armenian, Kalimi, and Zoroastrian) play a significant role. Family members used to consult with astrologers regarding the timing of various ceremonies in the past. In addition to religious occasions, some people also consider the stars and astronomy to be useful tools for determining the timing of their decisions and actions. A written agreement is prepared on a special piece of paper or notebook, and both parties and witnesses sign the document. The boy's family also presents a ring to the girl as a token of their appreciation. As part of this solemn ceremony, the bride's family treats the groom's family and his family with tea, syrup, sweets, and dinner.

3. Engagement

Following the initial arrangements for the marriage, a celebration called "engagement" is held in which the groom's family presents the bride with gifts, including an engagement ring. It's one of the most important marriage customs Iranians have inherited from the past. As an example, in Ferdowsi's Shahnameh, after "Zal" obtains his father's and the king's consent to marry Rudabeh, he sends her gifts and an engagement ring to the bride.

Sending a gift to the bride is considered one of the most important elements of the marriage ceremony in Shahnameh. Gifts such as ornaments, carpets, fabrics, cash, golden cradles, and even maids and slaves were often sent to the groom both at the time of the marriage and when the bride was brought to the groom's home. Ferdowsi gives the following example of these gifts in his poem about Siavash's marriage to Faringis (Jafari, 2022).

4. Marriage

Marriage involves a number of rituals, including the wedding ceremony. In addition to cultural, ethnic, and religious differences, political, economic, and social status of the bride and groom, as well as their families, play a role in how the wedding ceremony is conducted. According to Islamic jurisprudence, the recitation of the marriage text in Arabic is a necessary ceremony and a requirement for the validity of the marriage, therefore, usually clerics or those who are proficient in conducting this ceremony are invited to participate in the marriage ceremony as representatives of the bride. Traditionally, this ceremony was performed at the bride's house and before she leaves for her new house, in accordance with the ritual of the couple. The bride and groom sit on the sofa wearing the most beautiful clothes, accepting the commitments and responsibilities of the beginning of a joint life, according to traditional customs. The wedding table symbolizes the beginning of a joint life. During this ceremony, both parties' families and their guests are present. A cohabitation relationship culminates in the recitation of the marriage contract by the groom, the celebration of the marriage, and the signing of this cohabitation contract with the most beautiful form of traditional, religious, and legal customs. It is not uncommon for families to hold wedding ceremonies in hotels and halls or even in their own homes, and then register them in the marriage registry.

Others may choose to hold their marriage ceremony at the official marriage registry office. In most parts of Iran, the bride's family pays all expenses related to the wedding reception.

⟨Figure 1⟩ The wedding table is decorated with a copy of the Quran, flowers, fruits and symbolic food. A family life officially begins here.

It is common for families to hold the wedding ceremony a few months or even a few years after the wedding ceremony. At this time, both families invite each other to parties, and the bride and groom exchange gifts on various occasions, including holidays and celebrations. In addition, the bride's family is busy preparing the home appliances and furniture, while the groom's family is trying to cover the wedding party's expenses and provide housing. The program also provides boys and girls with the opportunity to get to know each other more closely. There is no doubt that if they are experiencing insoluble differences during this time, they prefer to

<Figure 2> Decoration of the wedding table

separate immediately and not to hold a wedding ceremony.

5. Taking the home appliances and furniture to the bride's house

Several days prior to the wedding ceremony and after the bride's family has taken and arranged all the living things and facilities at the bride and groom's residence, the time comes for the wedding ceremony to take place. The ladies of the bride's and groom's families are invited to attend this ceremony in order to view the place where the bride and groom live together and their living facilities. As part of this ceremony, all the living things of the bride, including her jewelry, are displayed to the family, and the guests also present gifts to the bride. Today, this ceremony is rarely performed.

In the story of Shahnameh, the bride's family, who are mostly kings or nobles of the court, when sending the girl to the bride's new house, they bring a detailed home appliances and furniture with him. In addition to hundreds of servants, dozens of camels, thousands of horses and camels, silk cloths, war equipment, etc., this dowry is carried behind the bride when she travels to the groom's home.

Historically, the amount and variety of dowry items have been directly related to the social status of the bride and groom's families. As a result, some families cannot provide dowry for their daughters, and so they marry their daughters without dowry. As mentioned in the story of Bahramgur and the miller, when Bahram asks the miller, why have you not married your daughters? The miller replies that he is poor and has no dowry to give to her daughters, therefore Bahram marries them out of chivalry (Jafari, 2022, pp. 5-9).

6. Hanabandan

A Hanabandan ceremony is a kind of farewell ceremony for the bride's paternal family the night before her wedding. In this ceremony, the ladies of the bride's family gather and celebrate and at the end of the night, they put henna on the bride's palms in a traditional way.

〈Figure 3〉 Creating a beautiful work of art with henna

7. Wedding ceremony and bridal make-up

The wedding ceremony is the most important and most mag-
nificent celebration of the union of the bride and groom as well
as the beginning of the couple's joint and independent lives together. Makeup for the bride is one of the wedding ceremonies.
An important custom of marriage that has survived from the past is
this custom. As per Ferdowsi, in the past, the bride was decorated
with jewels, crowns, silk clothes, cosmetics, and perfumes by her
mother. During the wedding of Zal and Rudabe, Rudabe's mother
Sindokht is in charge of her makeup.

Unlike today, when the wedding dress is usually white, in the ancient period, the wedding dress was usually made of silk and yellow or red, and nowadays some parts of Iran, including the Kalhor tribe in Kermanshah province, and the Turkmen people, wear wedding dresses that are red, yellow, or green in color. In Sistan, there is more to the fabric than gold-embroidered atlases or cream-embroidered fabric with vibrant red and pink colors or bright colors.

For the wedding ceremony, the guests of the couple's families, acquaintances, and friends are invited to enjoy a variety of sweets, syrups, and fruits as part of the celebration. The ceremony provides an opportunity for both sides to meet and visit their families, friends and acquaintances. At the end of the reception, the guests congratulate the bride and groom and wish them a happy future. Following the ceremony, the bride and groom are escorted to their respective homes by their families and close friends.

The bride is also taken to the groom's house in Mahd Zarin as part of another wedding ritual in Shahnameh. Golden cradles, which are sometimes prepared for the bride's companions, are usually adorned with special decorations. When Maryam, the daughter of the Roman Emperor, married Khosrow Parviz, her golden cradle was adorned with royal jewels.

At the weddings of Bahram Gur with girls from the common people of the society, this golden nursery is seen, and of course, the purpose of the golden nursery is to adorn it with yellow flowers.

There are times when the bride travels from another city or country to the bride's home country and the groom's home country. The ceremony also included a farewell and welcome. According to the Shahnameh, when the bride leaves for the groom's house accompanied by a caravan of gifts, slaves, and maids, her father, and some elders and soldiers accompany her for a distance and then return to her home. When the King of China sends his daughter to Anushirvan, he accompanies her to Jihun's shore. The elders of the court and the groom's family prepare the city and welcome the bride in the groom's hometown. "Azin" or "Ayin" are small domes (tents) that are placed on roofs and high places, and when the bride's caravan or any other welcome party passes through these tents, gold, saffron, musk, or flowers are poured on their heads. By doing so, the sweet smell of the bride fills the entire room. As he enters the city, he hears the sound of music everywhere and is showered with fragrant and precious materials (Jafari, 2022, pp. 5-9).

8. Patakhti

Women from both families attend the "Patekhti" celebration the day after the wedding ceremony and present gifts as a way of congratulating the newlyweds on their first night together.

9. Inviting the Bride to Groom's family after marriage

It is common for close relatives and acquaintances of the bride and groom to invite the newlyweds for a meal or lunch to express friendship and intimacy and to provide space for future visits. In this program, gifts are also given to the bride.

And as the last point: among the developments in recent years are group weddings and metaverse weddings. To encourage young people to get married, some associations and charities organize mass weddings for them. But there are different reasons for holding a Metaverse wedding ceremony. While some brides and grooms hold their wedding ceremonies in metaverse due to the fact that they live far away from their families and relatives, or to comply with protocols and regulations related to social distance and control of epidemic diseases, some others turn to this kind of ceremony just out of fashion and innovation.

⟨Figure 4⟩ Metaverse marriage

References

Al-Jawahiri, M. 1981. *Jawahir al-Kalam 29*. Beirut : Dar Ihya al-Turath al-Arabi.

Arberry (translated by). 2015. *The Holy Quran*. Tehran : Quran publishing center.

Farhange Tafahum. 2022, 9 14. *Marriage Registration*. Retrieved from Farhange Tafahum:: https://farhangetafahom.ir/%D8%AB%D8%A8%D8%AA-%D9%86%DA%A9%D8%A7%D8%AD-%D9%88-%D8%A7%D8%B2%D8%AF%D9%88%D8%A7%D8%AC-%D8%AF%D8%B1-%D8%AF%D9%81%D8%A7%D8%AA%D8%B1-%D8%A7%D8%B3%D9%86%D8%A7%D8%AF-%D8%B1%D8%B3%D9%85%DB%8C/

Ganjavi, N. 2022, 9 7. *Ganjavi, Nizami;*. Retrieved from Haft Paykar : https://ganjoor.net/nezami/5ganj/7peykar

Jafari, M. 2022. Shahnameh. In Editors, *The Great Islamic Encyclopedia*. Tehran : Center for the Great Islamic Encyclopedia. Retrieved from The Great Islamic Encyclopedia.

The Constitution of the Islamic Republic of Iran. 2022, 9 15. *The Constitution of the Islamic Republic of Iran*. Retrieved from Office of the President, IR. Iran : https://www.nicc.gov.ir/2016-10-31-15-10-28.html

UN Family Rights. 2022, 10 3. *The most basic human right is the right to a family*. Retrieved from UN Family Rights : https://unfamilyrightscaucus.org/

United Nation Organization. 2022, 10 3. *Universal Declaration of Human Rights*. Retrieved from UNO. : https://www.un.org/en/about-us/universal-declaration-of-human-rights

Image Source

⟨Figure 1⟩ https://www.honardarkhane.com/wp-content/uploads/2022/01/Decorate-the-bride-Quran.jpg

⟨Figure 2⟩ https://gahar.ir/%D8%A2%D9%85%D9%88%D8%B2%D8%B4-%DA%A9%D8%A7%D9%85%D9%84-%D8%AA%D8%B2%DB%8C%DB%8C%D9%86-%D8%B3%D9%81%D8%B1%D9%87-%D8%B9%D9%82%D8%AF/⟩

⟨Figure 3⟩ https://www.pinterest.com/pin/766034217880107839/?mt=login

⟨Figure 4⟩ https://www.iranicard.ir/blog/what-is-a-metaverse-marriage/

6부

고대 그리스의 결혼
(Marriage in Ancient Greece)

세바스티안 밀러(Sebastian Müller)

(부산외대 지중해지역원)

Marriage and accompanying wedding ceremonies are social institutions that can be observed in most cultures around the world. A marriage is not only the union of two people, it is an event that pertains to their own families and to wider social groups of their community. Modern perceptions of weddings are often based on romantic love and thus the free choice of a partner which was quite different from the motivations in ancient times. Traditionally, a wedding is a socially approved way to have legitimate offspring and heirs. Although this perception may have changed in modern times, a wedding is accompanied with a change of social status until today. It is often seen as a natural stage in one's lifetime. Thus, weddings are often conceptualized as so-called 'rites of passage' that mark an important life-changing event and a transformation of those who undergo the rites. Wedding ceremonies in the past and present differ around the world. Ancient societies in the Mediterranean had very sophisticated wedding rituals and performances that served several functions at the same time; some of them seem to play a role up to the present. As a public event, a wedding was always an opportunity of the families involved to demonstrate their power and wealth. The participation in the celebrations created dependencies and offered a stage for the host to influence the public opinion. Additionally the participants also had the role to confirm and testify that the wedding took place and that husband and wife were indeed married in line with the required rituals. This was specifically important in societies that did not use a central register for recording this kind of matters.

The present chapter offers a description of the wedding ceremonies in ancient Greece. First, a short introduction into the Greek world is given, followed by a few explanations about our knowledge of this time. After that the wedding customs of the ancient Greeks are introduced as much as they can be reconstructed based on the available information.

The World of the Ancient Greeks

Before describing the wedding ceremony and rituals of the ancient Greeks, it seems to be necessary to take a look at the world and circumstances in which these people lived. The main land of Greek people is located in a specific area of the Mediterranean Sea, known as the Aegean Sea (fig. 1) which belongs in modern times to the countries of Greece and Turkey. Although particular traits that were important in Greek culture have their beginnings already in the Bronze Age (c. 3000-1000 B.C.), the actual development to Greek society, as famously represented in the classical period (5th to 4th centuries B.C.), started at the beginning of the first millennium B.C. However, the first traces of a Greek dialect go back to the later Bronze Age in the Peloponnese and Central Greece which was home to the Mycenaean civilization. The Mycenaean people were organized in centralized polities that developed around fortified palace-sites. They had a writing system, constructed monumental structures and engaged in trade connections within the eastern

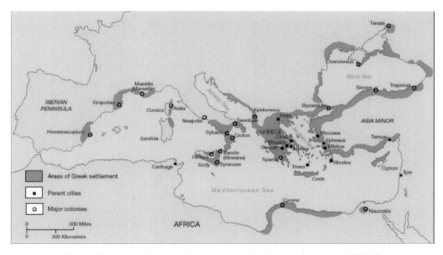

〈Figure 1〉 Areas of Greek settlement in the Mediterranean around 500 B.C.

Mediterranean and beyond.[1] As this civilization collapsed at the end of the Bronze Age together with other advanced states in the eastern Mediterranean region, a decline in many fields of people's life is observable. Nevertheless, this situation gave space for something new, the development of ancient Greek civilization.

After the monumental walls and palaces of the Bronze Age were destroyed or abandoned, the people in the Aegean region first lived in smaller village communities which grew together over several generations into larger cities. These cities developed to full-fledged states, known as *polis* which all had their own political alignment and constitution.[2] For Greek people the city was the central reference to their identity and the citizens of even neighboring cities or *poleis* were perceived as foreigners. A sense of community was, however, present due to the language as Greek people would call everyone who did not speak Greek a barbarian - for the language of foreign people would sound like 'bar bar' to their ears. A commonly shared religion with the pantheon of the twelve gods and goddesses who were believed to reside on mount Olympus in the northwest of the Aegean region was another strong connecting element.[3] Festivals in

---

1   Castleden, Rodney. *Mycenaeans*. London: Routledge, 2005.

2   Hansen, Mogens Herman. *Polis. An Introduction to the Ancient Greek City-State*. Oxford: Oxford University Press, 2006.

3   Guthrie, William, *The Greeks and Their Gods*. Boston: Beacon Press, 1971.

honor of the gods such as the Olympic Games which were held according to the historical tradition for the first time in 776 B.C. were events in which all Greeks, no matter where they lived, tried to participate. Historical events like the battles against the Achaemenid Empire or the Peloponnesian War[4] contributed to the emergence of a Greek, or more precisely, Panhellenic identity.[5]

The numerous islands in the Aegean motivated the people who lived in this area to engage in the construction of ships and to develop advanced navigation skills from an early period. With this knowledge, following the example of other seafaring people, prominently the Phoenicians from the coast of the Levant, the Greeks were able to navigate through the entire Mediterranean Sea. This brought them in contact with other cultures and civilizations along the shore and opened new opportunities for trade and other exchanges. Outposts that were created for trade purposes and newly established settlements often developed into full-fledged cities on their own in different regions of the Mediterranean such as Sicily, southern Italy, southern France and Spain, or in the Black Sea (fig. 1). The presence of Greek settlers in an area had a profound impact on the local people but also the Greek communities were influenced by the

---

4   Abulafia, David, *The Great Sea. A Human History of the Mediterranean*. Oxford: Oxford University Press, 2011, 132-137.

5   Ancient Greek people would refer to themselves as Hellenes.

cultures they encountered. Important trade goods of Greek origin were wine, olive oil, clothing and pottery. Latter was produced in dedicated workshops in different places with a distinctive style. Ancient Greek people created a wide range of pottery types which all had a dedicated function in daily life and in extraordinary events like religious celebrations, funerals and weddings. More elaborate and costly pottery vessels were also painted, in the classical period with scenes of festivals, celebrations, performances, mythological events and many more. Therefore, pottery is an important source for understanding the life of ancient Greek people. Some workshops were specialized in producing vessels for export and they would take the preference for particular scenes among their foreign customers into account.

As mentioned above, each Greek city was its own state with unique traditions. Although the gods and goddesses of the Greek pantheon were respected by all people in the Aegean, each city focussed specifically on the worship of one of the divine beings. Bigger differences could exist in the political constitution of the city-states. Whilst some of them were ruled by a single person or by a group of influential individuals, others were democracies involving the citizens of the state in the process of political decision-making.[6]

---

6   *Hansen, Polis*, 109-110.

The political system of a city-state was usually not fixed and thus it was possible that different ways of rule would emerge from time to time. The most famous example of a democratic city-state is Athens. The Attic democracy which underwent several constitutional changes and was interrupted by short periods of autocratic rulership, has been considered as the origin of democracies in Europe and other parts of the world. Democracy in the understanding of ancient Greek people was, however, not inclusive, since only the male citizens from a particular age were allowed and obligated to participate in political decisions. Women, people under a particular age, foreigners, slaves and others were generally excluded.[7] Citizenship and thus the right to have a voice in the matters of the state was only granted to citizens' children who were born from a socially approved marriage. The participation in political assemblies and debates but also in the numerous festivals and rites dedicated to the divine entities required a huge amount of disposable time. This was only possible because of the wide distribution of serfdom and slavery which is one of the dark sides of ancient Mediterranean civilizations. It can be assumed that a number of technological, artistic, philosophical and other intellectual achievements of the ancient Greeks were made on the backs of the large workforce of slaves.

---

7   Abulafia, David, *The Great Sea. A Human History of the Mediterranean*. Oxford: Oxford University Press, 2011, 138.

The settlement of Greek people in the Mediterranean from the 8th century B.C. and the favor of everything Greek by the Romans who started to expand their territory to other regions of the Mediterranean from the 3rd century B.C. had a profound impact on the profusion of elements of Greek culture. Some of these elements have survived in a noticeable way until modern times.

Sources

When dealing with a society that existed 2500 years ago, one of the first questions is certainly how we can know anything from this time as there is no way to experience the celebrations in person and to talk to the involved people. For ancient Greek society we are in the lucky situation to have remains of the material culture, visual art and historical sources. Each of them provide unique and important information which in best case confirm and complement each other. The elements of ancient Greek weddings are covered in all of these sources to a certain degree and thus it is possible to reconstruct most of the constituent parts of the ceremonies. There is one problem though that needs to be taken into account: the largest part of available sources refers to the biggest and in many aspects most influential city-state of Athens. As mentioned above,

Greek city-states had their own customs and unique cultural traits that distinguished them from each other. Using the examples from one city-state such as Athens to make conclusions about the customs of the entire ancient Greek world is thus very problematic. For the following descriptions it is, therefore, important to keep in mind that the available evidence is limited, fragmented and not representative of individual cities. Additionally, the available sources stem from different times, most of them, however, from the 4th and 3rd century B.C.[8] Some of the information is only derived from much later sources that refer to older works. Considering a timespan of several hundred years, we have to assume that some of the elements that belonged to the wedding ceremony changed over time in ancient Greek society.

Historical sources, meaning written accounts from people who lived in antiquity, often represent only a specific fraction of the ancient communities, namely famous, powerful and rich people. Information about most members of the society can only be retrieved through archaeological sources, which offer insights into very specific activities and events, but not into the details and sequences of the wedding. Visual art, for instance represented in pot-

---

8   Oakley, John H. and Rebecca H. Sino. *The Wedding in Ancient Athens*. Madison: The University of Wisconsin Press, 1993, 5-7.

tery paintings, is a very important source of information.[9] Here it is just important to keep in mind that the depicted scenes show a very idealized image. Moreover, several steps of the wedding ritual can be shown in one scene, often supernatural beings and mythological characters are added as reference to traditions that were very well understood by the ancient people but which remain enigmatic for the modern observer.

In sum, based on the available sources it is only possible to give a basic outline of the wedding celebrations and we always have to consider that individual cases may have deviated from this basic, perhaps in some regard ideal, conception quite significantly.

The Perception on Marriage in Ancient Greece

As mentioned above, marriage in ancient Greece had several social functions. One of its central aspects was the foundation of a family unit or household and related to that to have offspring of legitimate status which would be the legal heirs and who acquired the rights of citizenship in the city-state.[10] Latter was very important

---

9   Ibid.

10   Ibid. 9.

since children born from connections outside of legal marriages would be excluded from important rights. In the famous democracy of Classical Athens, as mentioned above, only those members of the society were allowed to participate in the communal decision-making who were full-fledged citizens of the polis. The way how the citizens could participate in politics sheds light on other aspects of society, as for example only males were accepted as politicians and voters. Women were officially excluded from the process and this discrimination against the female members of the society is also manifest in many aspects of the wedding.

Generally, it can be stated that in ancient Greece as well as in other societies of the Mediterranean, there was a clear inequality at the expense of the female members. Women, although having considerable power in the domestic sphere, were excluded from the public and the ideal was that married women should stay as much at the house as possible.[11] Women were seen as subordinates to their husbands, fathers or other male guardians who would make decisions on their behalf. It seems that there was often a significant age-gap between bride and groom which clearly contributed to the solidification of the power-difference between both partners.[12]

---

11   Alwang, Camryn, "Marriage and abduction myths of the ancient Greeks: a means of reinforcing the patriarchy." *Honor's Project.* 2021, 4-8.

12   It seems, however, that marriage was not seen as favorable when the age-gap was too

Another aspect that highlights the passive role of the bride is the ambivalent meaning of the ancient Greek word for marriage: *gamos*, as this can also be translated as 'abduction'. One of the oldest and probably most prominent cases in this regard is the abduction of the beautiful Helen by Paris, the son of the king of Troy, which was, as narrated by Homer, the cause for the Troyan war.

A dramatic consequence of the wedding was that the bride would leave the house of her parents and become a member of the husband's household. How she was treated under the aegis of her mother-in-law and other family members in the husband's household depended certainly on individual circumstances.

In any case, the disparities of the genders were manifest in all steps for the preparation and in the performances of the wedding rituals.

Before the wedding

Ancient Greek people considered the ideal month for marriages to be *Gamelion*, which is around January/February, as this was the same time as the marriage of the king of the Greek gods Zeus and

---

big. See Oakley and Sino, *The Wedding in Ancient Athens*, 10.

Hera, the goddess of women, marriage and the household, was celebrated.[13] This does, of course, not mean that wedding ceremonies took place only at that time. Additionally, the days of the full moon were seen as a good point in time.

The wedding celebration was normally planned to take place for three days, but celebrations that took less or more time are known as well. The three days represent the different stages of the wedding process with the first day called *proaulia*, the wedding day *gamos* and the third day *epaulia* which can be roughly translated as: 'before (pro) and after (ep) passing the night'.[14]

The actual wedding or *gamos*, as ancient Greek people would term it, was precluded – in some cases several years before the event – with a marriage agreement, the *engye* (literally: "placed in the hand"), between the bridegroom and the father of the bride.[15] If both parties were content with the conditions of the union, they would seal their agreement with a handshake. From this time on the couple was engaged which did, however, as far as we know, not result in the establishment of a closer relationship between the

---

13   Oakley and Sino, *The Wedding in Ancient Athens*, 10.

14   Mason, Casey, "The Nuptial Ceremony of Ancient Greece and the Articulation of Male Control Through Ritual." *Classics Honors Projects*, Paper 5, 2006, 20.

15   Alwang, "Marriage and abduction myths of the ancient Greeks", 17.

future wife and her husband. The opinion of the bride was of secondary importance anyway, since her father or male guardian was allowed to make these kinds of decisions without her approval.

It is difficult to estimate the number of marriages that were decided and done without taking the opinion of the bride into account, we may assume this depended on the individual situation at her parental home. Without personal accounts it is not easy for us in modernity to comprehend the thoughts and feelings of people in ancient times. It is possible that most women in the ancient Greek world did not consider it as their task or personal matter to choose a husband on their own, as this was never an option offered to them.

The customs and rituals that had to be observed before and during the wedding were quite complex and additionally the bride was expected to present herself to her husband and the audience of the wedding in the most elaborate and flawless way. Dealing with the bridal make-up and dress was already a task that required full attention, so much so that the bride's parents would hire a woman, known as *nympheutria*, who was in charge to oversee all the matters related to the bride.[16] The bridegroom was also required to

---

16   Oakley and Sino, *The Wedding in Ancient Athens*, 16.

observe particular rituals but it seems that it was not necessary to hire someone to assist him with that.

In ancient Greece the gods and goddesses were omnipresent and part of daily life. People believed that the divine beings had a strong interest in their doings. Moreover the gods could become displeased easily with serious consequences on the subjects of their wrath. Homer's narration of the Troyan war and the surrounding events are full of examples that describe how gods and goddesses interfered in human matters and how their actions were driven by affection or revenge. Therefore, appeasement and getting the favor of the gods through sacrifices was an integral part of people's routine. This was even more necessary in phases of transition from one stage of life to another such as the wedding, because the correct and complete performance of the rituals was seen as a precondition for a successful marriage. Visual art suggests that particular gods and goddesses were considered to be present at the wedding ceremony which made it even more necessary to follow the required rituals as closely as possible in order to keep getting the favor of the divine beings.

The wedding sacrifices were called *proteleia*. Gifts had to be made by the bride to the goddess Artemis, who was among others the protector of children, and to Aphrodite, who represented sexual love. The former was specifically necessary as the status of the bride would change in the perception of ancient Greek people with the wedding from child to adult.[17] Thus Artemis had to be appeased. A ritual by the bride in connection to the wedding preparations is demonstrating this tradition symbolically, as she would offer child clothes and toys to the goddess. This example also shows the psychological meaning of these rituals for the performing person, as the bride would be enabled to let go mentally of her childhood by giving the objects that indicate her status as a child to a divine entity.

Based on local customs and other circumstances, sacrifices had to be offered to other gods and goddesses as well. The required sacrifices were set by tradition and also by the economic abilities of the involved families. Processions that displayed the offerings to the public are a frequent theme in ancient visual art. In connection with music, dances, the singing of particular songs and the display of the offerings to the gods, this was an effective means to convey the message about an imminent wedding to the community and - equally important for families of power - to show off their economic potential to the public.

---

17   Ibid. 14.

As mentioned above, the rituals were also a means of mental preparation for a new role and status in the community after the ceremony. Aside from sacrifices and offerings in order to propitiate divine beings, a very important wedding preparation for bride and groom was to take a ritual bath. The idea was not only to clean oneself in the physical sense but also spiritually and to absorb the life-giving properties of water.[18] The water for the bath was taken from a special source, often a river, and it was carried in a particular vessel called a *loutrophoros* (bathwater carrier) (fig. 4). The water was carried by a specifically appointed child in a procession guided by an *aulos* (double flute) -player with dancers and accompanied by other people.[19]

Since a wedding was an extraordinary event for the directly involved people, there was - as today in such situations - a special recognition for the adornment and dress of the main protagonists. After the bath the broom was dressed with a very thin cloak, the *himation*, and he had a wreath on his head made of different plants which were considered to have specific effects on the body as aphrodisiac or to enhance fertility. The groom would also use a

---

18   Ibid. 15-16.

19   Ibid.

perfume that included myrrh.[20]

The bride wore a *chiton*, a kind of tunic, and a *himation*, a cloak, preferably in purple color and a rich adornment including a necklace made of gemstones (fig. 2; 3). Purple was a very costly dye for clothes in antiquity due to the immense effort to yield the color from sea snails that each contain only a tiny amount of pigments. Additionally, the process to obtain the pigments was complicated and required specific facilities. In ancient times purple dye was produced and distributed by the Phoenicians, people who lived in city-states along the eastern Mediterranean coast. Purple color became synonymous with affluence and power which is why this color was reserved from medieval times for European royals and high officials of the church up to early modernity.

Purple was also the color of the goddess Aphrodite, whose realm the bride was about to enter through the marriage.[21] A dress that carried at least partly this color would be both a reference to the goddess and another indicator that the family of the bride was able to afford such an expensive clothing.

---

20   Ibid. 16.

21   Ibid.

⟨Figure 2⟩ Preparations for a wedding – ancient Greek ceramic painting.[22]

In addition to the clothes, the bride wore also special wedding sandals called *nymphides* and a crown, the *stephane*. The crown was occasionally made of metal, but consisted more often of plants with different meanings and references.[23] The bride was surrounded by the scent of her perfume that was similar to the unguent used by the groom made of myrrh. A veil was worn over the crown and

---

22 https://commons.wikimedia.org/wiki/File:Preparations_for_a_wedding_-_ancient_Greek_ ceramic_painting.jpg

23 Mason, "The Nuptial Ceremony of Ancient Greece", 28.

used by the bride to cover her face until she appeared in front of her soon-to-be husband for the unveiling ceremony.

Another part of the preparation for the wedding was the decoration of the houses of the bride and the groom. Branches of trees and garlands were used for this purpose.[24] It can be assumed that the used plants had a special meaning in regard to the wedding as well. The adorned facades would be another indicator to the public that a wedding ceremony was in process.

The wedding

After all the mentioned preparations were done the actual wedding could begin. Central part of the entire event was the wedding feast which was of utmost significance for the ancient Greek people. Similar to the important Greek institution known as *symposion*, the feast would include the consumption of wine, the ingestion of different kinds of food, music, recitations of poetry etc. Whilst the symposion was highly restrictive regarding the participants, women of status, for instance, were not allowed to attend their husbands to

---

24 Oakley and Sino, *The Wedding in Ancient Athens*, 21.

these important social events, in case of a wedding this restriction did not apply. Women and men were allowed to participate but they were seated separately from each other.[25] The participants were composed of the marrying couple's family members and friends. The number of guests that were hosted and the foods that were offered at this occasion were important indicators of a family's status within the community and their wealth. The place for the feast was either the house of the bride's family or that of the groom's family.[26]

The food was composed of a large variety of dishes among which meat was extensively offered, for this was a "remnant" from the previous sacrifices to the gods.[27] One distinctive wedding food was the *sesame*, a simple cake-like dish made of sesame seeds and honey which is still known in Greece as a snack or dessert called *pasteli*. Sesame was seen as a symbol for abundance and fertility. It was eaten by the marrying couple and the guests.

---

25 Ibid. 22.

26 Smith, Amy Claire, "The politics of weddings at Athens: an iconographic assessment." *Leeds International Classical Studies* 4 (1), 2005, 5.

27 Oakley and Sino, *The Wedding in Ancient Athens*, 23.

〈Figure 3〉 Terracotta lebes gamikos (round-bottomed bowl with handles and stand used in weddings), attributed to the Naples Painter, Greek, Attic.

〈Figure 4〉 Terracotta loutrophoros (ceremonial vase for water), ca. 400 B.C., Greek, Attic.

The feast was, as mentioned, accompanied by music and although this was a very common element, for the wedding special songs were played and sung by the participants. Their content was often to make fun of the bride and groom.[28] Dancing was also an integral element of weddings and it seems that dances were performed at different stages of the celebrations. As far as this can be ascertained from the visual art, people would dance in a row, similarly to the traditional *sirtaki*-dance that is a symbol of national identity for

---

28   Ibid. 23. Mason, "The Nuptial Ceremony of Ancient Greece", 34-35.

modern Greek people. In ancient times women and men did not dance together but the dancers were also not spatially separated from each other. Generally the dance was not only performed for entertainment, it had a deeper meaning as it was considered to be sacred and a necessary element of a wedding and other celebrations.[29]

The core event of the wedding ceremony was the *anakalypteria*, the moment of unveiling the bride.[30] There is different information when this happened but it seems that during the feast was the most common occasion as this part of the wedding required a number of witnesses. Until this moment the bride and groom did not see each other. The main part of the ritual is that the groom offered gifts, called *opteria* or *theoretra*, to the bride and she had to accept them. The gifts themself were seen as proof of the wedding – similar to the modern wedding ring – and the people attending the ritual would be able to testify that the wedding took place also by mentioning the different presents the bride received in course of the ceremony.[31]

For ancient Greek people the main part of the wedding was not so much the unveiling of the bride but her procession to the house

---

29 Oakley and Sino, *The Wedding in Ancient Athens*, 24-25.

30 Smith, "The politics of weddings at Athens", 6.

31 Oakley and Sino, *The Wedding in Ancient Athens*, 25.

of the groom. The procession was another occasion to inform the community about the ongoing wedding and it was the symbolic and spatial transfer of the soon-to-be wife to her new life. The procession consisted of family members and friends as well as musicians and other professionals. One aspect of this custom was to protect the bride and to make sure that she would arrive safe at the house of the groom's family.[32] Here the idea to have women always under the protection of the male family members plays the determining role. It was the special duty of the bride's mother to guide her daughter to the new home. She carried a torch that was lit with the fire from the hearth of the house which was a sacred place in each household. From paintings on pottery we know that the bride was driving in the procession in a cart (fig. 5) and that she traveled the distance covered with the veil. Beside her was a specifically appointed protector, the *paranymphos*, a person with a close relationship to the groom, and the above mentioned woman appointed by the bride's parents, the *nympheutria*.[33] The groom himself was part of the procession as well, but it seems that sometimes he traveled individually. The participants of the procession were divided by gender and age. They also did not just walk along,

---

32 Smith, "The politics of weddings at Athens", 6.

33 Oakley and Sino, *The Wedding in Ancient Athens*, 27.

they rather danced and sang. Music, singing and shouting would create a specific soundscape that informed also those people who were not directly present at the site that a wedding procession was in progress. Onlookers of the procession could shower leaves and blossoms on the bride and groom, similarly to modern customs to throw flowers or rice.

〈Figure 5〉 Painting on a terracotta lekythos (oil flask), ca, 550–530 B.C.

Finally, the procession arrived at the house of the groom where his mother was waiting in front of the door with a lit torch (fig. 5). The house was adorned with garlands and other ornaments to signify the arrival of a new family member. Entering the house was another critical moment in the transition process of the bride and it was necessary to introduce her properly with the right rituals. When the marrying couple stepped into the house they were showered with the *katachysmata* which "consisted of dates, coins, dried fruits, figs, and nuts",[34] all things that symbolized an affluent and well-

---

34 Oakley and Sino, *The Wedding in Ancient Athens*, 34.

maintained household.

The symbolic and spiritual center of the Greek house was the hearth. Bride and groom had to appear in front of the hearth or at least had to pass the fireplace before getting into the bridal chamber. A ritual that probably took place near the hearth is the offering of a *malon*, a quince or apple, to the bride and her eating it.[35] Although there are several meanings related to this activity, it is the ingestion of the food in the new house that transforms the bride into a member of the household.

After following all necessary rituals upon entering the house, the groom led his wife-to-be to the bridechamber, called *thalamos*. The central part of this room was a luxuriously adorned bed with fine linen and perfumed with scent.[36] Although the couple was expected to spend the night together in this bed, it is attested that another bed, the *parabustos*, was placed in the room allowing the bride or husband to sleep alone.[37] After the marrying couple had entered the room the door was closed and a guardian, the *thyroros*, was placed in front of it and would not allow anyone else to enter. The participants of the procession, particularly the friends of

---

35   Ibid. 35.

36   Mason, "The Nuptial Ceremony of Ancient Greece", 32. Oakley and Sino, *The Wedding in Ancient Athens*, 35.

37   Mason, "The Nuptial Ceremony of Ancient Greece", 32.

bride and groom, stayed nearby, singing and even knocking on the door. This was on one side to assure the bride that her relatives and friends were not far away, on a darker side it has been also mentioned that the noise was intended to cover possible screams of the bride for help.[38]

After the wedding

The next day after the bride and groom spent their first night to-gether was called the *epaulia* which is a reference to the gifts that were given to the newlywed bride and the groom. Based on the examples of visual art, the main recipient of the presents was the bride. Generally, this day was a continuation of the previous one with feasting, dancing and singing but the main event was a pro-cession in front of the married couple presenting gifts to them and also to the rest of the audience.[39] Again the way how the procession was outlined, which position the participants had etc. was all regu-lated by customs. Music was played, torches were carried. Although processions are a very common motif in ancient Greek artwork, it is

---

38 Oakley and Sino, *The Wedding in Ancient Athens*, 37.

39 Ibid. 38.

difficult to distinguish most of the goods that were actually presented to the couple. From literary sources that enumerate some of the
gifts it becomes obvious that a lot of them were dedicated to the
personal use of the bride. Mentioned are lidded vessels with different content, small vessels for unguents, chests, clothes and shoes,
bodycare products such as soap, perfume and herbs. It is very likely
that also pieces of adornment and smaller goods that were useful
for the bride were presented. At times the dowry which played an
important role as well was shown in this final procession.[40]

Probably on the same day or soon after, the husband had to
hold another feast, the *gamelia*, for his *phratria*, a kin-based group
of male citizens of a city-state. This event was again of high importance as the participants of this feast would all testify and confirm that husband and wife were properly married.[41] For this the
husband had to make clear that he had formed a new household,
called *oikos*, through the wedding. As mentioned above, this was of
utmost importance for the succession line, for making sure that the
offspring of the newlywed couple had the legal status of a citizen
and for solving any future legal issue in relation to the family.

---

40   Ibid.

41   Mason, "The Nuptial Ceremony of Ancient Greece", 54.

Other, household-related customs and rituals could follow on the last wedding day. In Athens, for instance, on the southern slope of the Acropolis was the location of an open air sanctuary of the Nymphe, a nature goddess who protected the wedding and the rites of marriage. At this sanctuary a huge amount of wedding vessels, for example *loutrophoroi*, and other objects related to the wedding have been unearthed.[42] It seems that the brides, maybe together with their husbands, sacrificed these objects in return to a successful wedding ceremony.

As mentioned above, the status of husband and wife changed after the wedding. Both had their traditional tasks and fields of activity. The house of wealthy Greek people was divided in a women- and men-quarter, the former was traditionally on the second floor, which made it easier to control the access to the female family members.[43] As has been the case in many patriarchal societies, giving birth to a healthy male child was the main priority of a married Greek woman.

---

42 Sabetai, Victoria, "The wedding vases of the Athenians: a view from sanctuaries and houses." *Mètis, Dossier : Des vases pour les Athéniens (Ve-IVe siècles avant notre ère)*, 2014, 51-79.

43 Walker, Susan, "Women and Housing in Classical Greece: the archaeological evidence." In *Images of Women in Antiquity*, edited by Averil Cameron and Amelie Kuhrt, 81-91. London: Routledge, 1983.

In case the marriage did not go well for one or both of the partners, it was possible to divorce. Husband and wife were both equally allowed to initiate the divorce but it seems that women had to reason their decision in front of an archon, a high-ranking magistrate in a number of city-states.[44] The husband could simply send his wife back to her family and with this act she was not a member of the husband's household anymore. It is unclear how many marriages were divorced in ancient Greece. Unlike in other cultures and societies the actual fact that a couple got divorced was not a huge problem or laden with shame. It depended more on the reasons for the divorce if one or both partners got the sympathy of their families and friends.

In sum

The wedding ceremony in ancient Greece was a matter of high importance. Marriage was seen as a natural step in the lifetime of a person and the main reason was to produce legitimate offspring. The children from a legally recognized marriage of two citizens of one of the numeros Greek city-states were granted citizenship

---

44   Cohn-Haft, Louis, "Divorce in Classical Athens". *The Journal of Hellenic Studies* 115, 1995, 4.

which was an important precondition to enjoy all the rights of the state. The rituals that composed the entire wedding ceremony were directed to appease the gods and goddesses who were believed to have a tremendous influence on people's life. Transitions from one status of life to the next played a role as well as making sure that the wedding and the ultimate goal, to have healthy and able heirs, would be fulfilled.

Another aspect of the wedding as a public event at least for powerful families was to demonstrate economic power and influence. Many aspects of the wedding such as the processions with music and dances, the feast for a larger group of guests and the adornment of the houses were additionally intended to inform as many people as possible in the community that the couple was legitimately married. This was necessary in order to have witnesses in case of legal disputes in which the legal status of children and of a wife was questioned.

Although many customs related to ancient Greek weddings appear to be very different from modern times, particular elements such as the unveiling of the bride, the feast and many smaller details have been adopted by other European cultures and some of them seem to have survived until modern times.

References

Abulafia, David. 2011. *The Great Sea. A Human History of the Mediterranean.* Oxford: Oxford University Press.

Alwang, Camryn. 2021. "Marriage and abduction myths of the ancient Greeks: a means of reinforcing the patriarchy." *Honor's Project.*

Castleden, Rodney. 2005. *Mycenaeans.* London: Routledge.

Cohn-Haft, Louis. 1995. "Divorce in Classical Athens". *The Journal of Hellenic Studies* 115. pp.1-14.

Cox, Cheryl A. 2011. "Marriage in Ancient Athens." In *A companion to families in the Greek and Roman worlds,* edited by Beryl Rawson. Chichester: Blackwell Publishing Ltd.

Guthrie, William. 1971. *The Greeks and Their Gods.* Boston: Beacon Press.

Hansen, Mogens Herman. 2006. *Polis. An Introduction to the Ancient Greek City-State.* Oxford: Oxford University Press.

Mason, Casey. 2006. "The Nuptial Ceremony of Ancient Greece and the Articulation of Male Control Through Ritual." *Classics Honors Projects.* Paper 5.

Oakley, John H. and Rebecca H. Sino. 1993. *The Wedding in Ancient Athens.* Madison: The University of Wisconsin Press.

Sabetai, Victoria. 2014. "The wedding vases of the Athenians: a view from sanctuaries and houses." *Mètis, Dossier : Des vases pour les Athéniens (Ve-IVe siècles avant notre ère).* pp.51-79.

Smith, Amy Claire. 2005. "The politics of weddings at Athens: an iconographic assessment." *Leeds International Classical Studies* 4 (1). pp. 1-32.

Walker, Susan. 1983. "Women and Housing in Classical Greece: the archaeological evidence." In *Images of Women in Antiquity,* edited by Averil Cameron and Amelie Kuhrt, 81-91. London: Routledge.

Image Source

⟨Figure 1⟩ https://en.wikipedia.org/wiki/File:Greek_Colonization.png

⟨Figure 2⟩ https://commons.wikimedia.org/wiki/File:Preparations_for_a_wedding_-_ancient_
Greek_ceramic_painting.jpg

⟨Figure 3⟩ https://www.metmuseum.org/art/collection/search/247460

⟨Figure 4⟩ https://www.metmuseum.org/art/collection/search/244821

⟨Figure 5⟩ Metmuseum, https://www.metmuseum.org/art/collection/search/254843

동지중해의 결혼 문화와 전통

초판인쇄 2022년 11월 30일
초판발행 2022년 11월 30일

지은이 지중해지역원
펴낸이 채종준
펴낸곳 한국학술정보(주)
주 소 경기도 파주시 회동길 230(문발동)
전 화 031-908-3181(대표)
팩 스 031-908-3189
홈페이지 http://ebook.kstudy.com
E-mail 출판사업부 publish@kstudy.com
등 록 제일산-115호(2000. 6. 19)

ISBN 979-11-6801-991-1 93920